THE COLORS OF MY SOUL

THE COLORS OF MY SOUL

A Journey Into Love

Viki Hart
&
Archangel Michael

BALBOA.
PRESS
A DIVISION OF HAY HOUSE

Balboa Press books may be ordered through booksellers or by contacting:

Balboa Press
A Division of Hay House
1663 Liberty Drive
Bloomington, IN 47403
www.balboapress.com
1-(877) 407-4847

Because of the dynamic nature of the Internet, any web addresses or links contained in this book may have changed since publication and may no longer be valid. The views expressed in this work are solely those of the author and do not necessarily reflect the views of the publisher, and the publisher hereby disclaims any responsibility for them.

The author of this book does not dispense medical advice or prescribe the use of any technique as a form of treatment for physical, emotional, or medical problems without the advice of a physician, either directly or indirectly. The intent of the author is only to offer information of a general nature to help you in your quest for emotional and spiritual well-being. In the event you use any of the information in this book for yourself, which is your constitutional right, the author and the publisher assume no responsibility for your actions.

Cover design by Courtney Starwolf Barry and Viki Hart.

ISBN: 978-1-4525-4047-4 (e)
ISBN: 978-1-4525-4048-1 (sc)
ISBN: 978-1-4525-4049-8 (hc)

Library of Congress Control Number: 2011918726

Printed in the United States of America

Balboa Press rev. date: 10/25/2011

To Mom & Michael

Thank you for offering me a life beyond my wildest dreams!

CONTENTS

THE COLORS OF MY SOUL

chapter one

The Forgetting Years

Recently, I have chosen an Angel as my life partner. It seems that the two of us have had a lifelong courtship, but no matter how hard I try, most of it I can't remember. I do have a few scattered memories of talking to God and the Angels as an infant playing in my crib, but these memories seem to be more the stuff of dreams and fantasies than the real world.

My human understanding of Angels began around age two. I would escape from the nursery after church services, lie down in the pews closest to the windows, and talk to the stained glass Angels until my mother found me and took me home. The Angels in these windows were over twelve feet tall and looked like humans with large white wings. My favorites were a smiling female Angel watching over a group of children playing at her feet and a very serious male Angel holding a sword.

As a child, I was never sure if this male Angel was protecting me or making sure that I was following the rules, but regardless of his purpose, when the sunshine streamed through these windows the Angels appeared to glow from within, and I felt the warmth of their light on my skin. I was enamored by the colors of their faces, eyes, hands, and clothes and was constantly looking for these stained glass beings in the world around me. Unfortunately, while I often felt the warmth of Angels, I rarely saw them. By the age of six, I had been taught that Angels lived far away in Heaven and I stopped trying to talk to them.

By the time I was a teenager, the loss of my special friends had left me lonely, depressed, anorexic, and convinced that I was unworthy of giving or receiving love. After completing college and a series of unsatisfying jobs, I moved from Illinois to Colorado and was estranged from my family for many years.

My first few years in Colorado were a reflection of my life in Illinois. I had a series of jobs that I hated, a romantic relationship that ended, anorexia that continued sporadically, and a condo that needed new carpeting. Then over Thanksgiving weekend of 1984, I adopted a dog from the Humane Society. Tippy had been abused, and while she was afraid of men and shy around women and children, she was totally devoted to me, and I soon felt the same about her.

For the first time in my life, I felt loved and capable of expressing my love. My desire to take care of this small creature triggered a new choice within me; I decided to stop smoking and heal my anorexia. While I weighed less than ninety pounds at the time, this decision was made with determination, not desperation. I wanted to live and be healthy in order to provide Tippy with the life she deserved!

As I strove to make Tippy happy, I realized that I wanted and deserved to be happy as well. By my late thirties, I was asking myself two simple questions: "Who am I?" and "Why am I here?" These questions eventually led me to a channeled reading of Archangel Michael. During this session, Michael challenged me about my beliefs, my family relationships, and my Divine Purpose. His energy felt very harsh and his words sliced into my heart. I decided that evening that I wanted nothing more to do with Angels!

However, I was intrigued with the idea of channeling and knew intuitively that I had the ability to connect with information from a source greater than myself, so I visited a gentle psychic who suggested that I start channel writing. She instructed me to sit down, quiet my mind, ask a question, and write without thinking. My first few lines were jibber jabber, but then strangely beautiful thoughts and ideas began to appear on the paper.

I knew these words weren't mine because they were positive and playful and I was, to say the least, neither of these things at the time. This written voice told me what foods my body needed, how to look at my job differently, and urged me to let go of the dream of my lost relationship in order to move on. While nothing outside of me changed—including the carpet in my condo—inside I was a different person.

As I continued to expand my study of metaphysics, I took some meditation classes to learn how to quiet my mind through focusing on my breath, but to be quite honest, most of the time I just got bored and started thinking about chocolate.

Then one night, I was relaxing in a hot bath, listening to new age music with only the soft flicker of candles lighting the room, when I heard a strange man's voice call out my name. The voice was loud and forceful and I was naked! I shot out of the tub, grabbed a towel, and sprinted to the phone to call 911. As I stood dripping in my living room with Tippy calmly looking up at me, I realized that there was no man in my condo; the voice was in my head!

For the next five to six years, my communications with this voice grew from one word, usually yes or no, to sentences, and then into paragraphs about any topic I asked about. I was never sure who or what this voice was or even if it was always the same voice, but the information was always soft and loving. I was even able to get information for other people, and over time, I learned to trust this information completely.

I can honestly say that it never once occurred to me that I might be talking to an Angel, even when friends and other psychics suggested that I had the ability to channel Archangel Michael (who of course was the last Angel I would ever consider talking to, let alone channel).

As I continued my journey of healing through the years, my mother was also reconnecting with her spirituality. In the late 1980s, Mom was diagnosed with breast cancer. During her first MRI, an Angel appeared and told her to seek treatment. She embraced this information with enthusiasm, and we thought the cancer had been eradicated until 1992 when she was diagnosed with her first brain tumor. My mother underwent a mastectomy, chemotherapy, two brain surgeries, and several rounds of radiation before deciding to stop treatment and allow the cancer to take its natural course.

I had just lost Tippy to cancer and was visiting my parents in Florida when the diagnosis of my mother's third brain tumor was made. My own guidance assured me that I needed to move to Florida and help care for her during the final months of her life. I arrogantly believed that I had completely healed myself and that I was doing this solely for my parents, out of a child's sense of duty and gratitude for all the financial support they had given me over the years.

I had no idea that my mother was about to reintroduce me to the love of my life, and forever change my Divine Path on Earth!

chapter two

My Mother's Final Gift

When the Angels brought me to Earth and placed me in my mother's arms, I was the essence of pure love and knew nothing of fear. Mom took on the immense responsibility of teaching me how to live in a world of fear and pulled out all the stops to assure that I would survive.

She taught me whom to fear, what to fear, the rules and limitations of fear, how to use anger, control, humor, repression, and denial to manage my fear, and at times, even took my hand and walked through my fear with me. Unfortunately, learning about fear on the Earth plane often required me to forget about love, and Mom assisted me with that process as well.

When Mom surrendered her own survival on the planet to God, she was released of all her responsibility to fear. During the final months of her life, Mom was free to remember who she was, why she was here, and how to live in complete unconditional love. She took full advantage of this opportunity and made the loving choice to teach me to do the same.

I never knew if the final brain tumor prevented Mom from making conscious connections with her Angels or if something else had intervened, but soon after I moved into my parents' home, I became her channel to the Angelic Realm as well as her physical caretaker. We spent our days quietly talking to Angels and finishing "her business" here on Earth. Each day, Mom would tell me the story of how her first Angel came to her. She would describe the glowing face of this Angel, its white wings, the flowers in its hair, and its soft flowing dress.

Mom looked for this Angel until the moment of her death, and while many other Angels assisted her in those final months, this Angel never returned. Over and over, my heart was broken by the yearning I heard in my mother's voice as she spoke of this Angel, and I wondered how such love could bring so much pain.

About two weeks before Mom died, I awoke to the sound of her voice calling to me in the middle of the night and immediately jumped out of bed and headed for her bedroom. I was not clairvoyant, but when I got to her door I clearly saw a huge golden Angel and Mother Mary standing beside the bed. Normally, I would have been thrilled to actually see an Angel, but a gut-wrenching fear that Mom had called me to say goodbye dampened the experience. I started to step into the room and Mary put her hand up to stop me.

I automatically stepped back and realized that four very large Angels had just surrounded me. I heard them say, *"Little One, your mother has asked that as her final gift to you, we take you into the Angelic Realm through her open doorway. Would you like to go?"*

Without thinking, I said, "Yes!" and was guided to my favorite chair on the lanai. In the moonless night, I saw a white light hovering above the trees in the distance and thought it must be a helicopter until it silently reached out and gently engulfed me in its essence.

As I relaxed into the white light, a gentle calm came over me. The fear that I had felt inside my gut dissolved, and soon my whole body just seemed to melt away as did all my human thoughts and feelings. In the timelessness of this light, I was safe, warm, and totally at peace.

The four Angels that had brought me into the light still surrounded me, and I was conscious of other groups of Angels surrounding other rather confused beings like myself. I felt the vibrations of hundreds, perhaps even thousands, of voices near me and knew that on Earth I might have been tempted to listen in, but here I was satiated with the sensations of a love that I had forgotten long ago in my journey on Earth. There was a fullness and completeness to my existence that even to this day my human mind cannot comprehend. I knew this place was where Mom was going and it was time to let her go, allow her to end her struggle and pain, and melt into this light. This was home!

Or so I thought! Suddenly, my four Angels opened an archway directly before me revealing a mass of rapturous ribbons of consciousness. This was a realm in which Divine Love expressed itself as the pure essence of vibrating color. I actually felt the individual strands of color as they flowed in and out of each other creating infinite forms and experiences before me, and my energy exploded in joy as I realized—this was my stained glass world!

My joy propelled me into the Angelic Realm and I instantly began to vibrate as an essence of blue. This sensation intensified my joy because blue had always been my favorite color, and I realized that through all of my forgetting on Earth, I had somehow retained the knowledge of my eternal existence. In contrast to the duality created by my fears on Earth, my Angelic essence resonated wholly in the fluid, flexible cohesiveness of Divine Love.

As I expanded further into my essence, I experienced a shift in my vibration to that of purple, then yellow, green, orange, pink, black, red, white, fuchsia, lilac, aqua, and on and on through every hue and shade of all the colors that exist on Earth and even more that don't, until I finally realized that I had no beginning or end. This sudden awareness of my infinity allowed me to rest in each color as I experienced its lifetime, knowledge, and wisdom.

I was then able to tap into the knowledge of how all my colors were woven together and realized that my Soul is much more than just the sum of my individual experiences and lifetimes. My Divine essence exists outside of time, allowing expressions of love to ripple outwards in all directions. Each time I express love on Earth, a vibration of love radiates through every color of my soul, expanding both my individual strand and the Angelic Realm. I immediately realized that it is this expansion of the Angelic Realm that makes humans as important to the Angels as the Angels are to humans.

As the love within my strand expanded to overflowing, I became aware of the strands surrounding me. The tiniest awareness of another strand allowed me to melt into it and access not only all the knowledge of our joint creations, but those experiences of the strand that did not include me.

As I began to melt into more and more strands, I became aware of the infinite combinations of our connections in the Angelic Realm, and I was able to move my consciousness anywhere in this realm instantly. It was exciting and blissful meeting all those old friends and relatives that had crossed over in this lifetime and reuniting with many more that shared experiences with other colors of my soul. In the Angelic Realm it is natural for me to BE individualized while simultaneously in the oneness of all that is.

My four Angels soon began to call my consciousness back to them, and while I wanted to keep flying, no matter how hard I tried I kept ending up right back where I started. Finally, I just gave up and began to focus on what was in front of me.

In that moment, Archangel Michael came forward and showed himself to me. The softness of his love flowed through me like warm sunlight, and I instantly understood that Archangel Michael was the oneness of all the shades, tints, and hues of blue that exist in the Angelic Realm, including mine, and I had to ask, "Michael, how could I have forgotten you?"

"Little One, the Angelic Realm cannot be explained in the physical realm, and as you have just discovered, once in the Angelic Realm,

no explanation is needed. When you enter into human form on Earth, you embrace the boundaries and limitations of your realm. This requires you to forget the infinite, eternal energy of your being in order to focus on the experiences of Earth. Your forgetting is an expression of Divine Love and is one of the most painful experiences a human can endure.

"Your path on Earth has now reached the moment of remembering, and your mother's gift has brought you back home to awaken your human consciousness to the love of your Divine essence."

Michael then had me focus on other strands and I remembered the greens of Archangel Raphael, the whites of Archangel Gabriel, the blacks of Archangel Uriel, the pink and reds of Archangel Ariella, and on and on. Michael also connected me with the Reiki Angel that I knew as Ren So May, and while she appeared to be about five feet tall and emerald green on Earth, in the Angelic Realm, her green and gold strands expanded into infinity. I was also greeted by a number of other individual and grouped strands that serve as Guardian Angels, Joy Angels, Abundance Angels, Healing Angels, and Angels with every function one could possibly imagine.

As I became more comfortable with the vibrations of the Angelic Realm, my four Angels escorted me to another area where I noticed a small spot that aroused my curiosity. This energy was very different from the expansive consciousness that I had encountered up to then. There appeared to be a boundary around it, and the strands within this area were denser, more rigid, and seemed to be moving very slowly. When I touched it with my consciousness I knew—this was Earth!

For a brief moment, I knew Earth's Divine Plan, how it was created, what each individual was doing on the planet, and how each life consciousness on Earth interacted with all others. I could see both its individualized strands of life consciousness and its oneness flowing through the creation of linear time. It was brilliant and amazing!

Michael explained, *"The Angelic Realm is the origin of Earth and its physical universe, as well as all the realms that support and interact with your planet. All of the souls that take individualized form on Earth are merely extensions of their energy in the Angelic Realm and are collectively known as the 'One Soul of Earth.' Since Earth exists within the Angelic Realm, our energy is constantly aware of and supporting all life consciousness on your planet. It's like a two-way mirror, the Angels can see you, but you cannot see them."*

Michael then guided my focus to several other realms that connected into our physical universe. There were many different types of realms, but my favorites included the Fairy Realm, the Celestial Realm, and several realms known as the Underworlds. My work on Earth in previous years with Shamans, Buddhists, Reiki Masters, and other metaphysical practitioners had brought me into contact with these realms, so it was fun to see them from another perspective.

"Little One, each realm in the One Soul of Earth is created by slowing the energy of the Angelic Realm, and creating a specific range of vibratory frequencies. In addition, each individual realm is separated from other realms by an intermediary energy field, which acts as a veil between them. The white light that you entered prior to coming into the Angelic Realm was one of those veils.

"Meditation, prayer, and ritual can alter the vibratory frequency of an individual consciousness in any given realm for short periods of time, allowing it to pierce the veil and see beyond its world. There are even doors and windows that exist in each veil to allow such connections to be made. However, the veils were created to allow life consciousness to fully focus on and experience the world they have chosen to enter."

I asked Michael how we enter the Earth plane and he softly said, *"The answer to that question will have to wait. When your consciousness is sped up to the vibratory frequency needed to enter the Angelic Realm, the energy in your physical body is also increased. This can greatly stress and even alter your human body, so your visit to the Angelic Realm must be limited to protect your existence on Earth."*

The Angels then gently guided me back into my body and I was greeted by the first rays of a new dawn. I felt an almost stifling humidity on my skin and within my lungs for an instant, and then an overwhelming sense of gratitude and joy filled my body.

I stood up and walked to my mother's bedroom door where my parents were sleeping. Mother Mary and the Golden Angel had disappeared from sight. In that moment, I opened my heart and created a new relationship of eternal love and gratitude with my mother.

As I slowly walked back to my bedroom, the experience of my visit to the Angelic Realm was already slipping from my human consciousness, and I intuitively knew that in a few hours I would once again be lost in my forgetting. Yet, I stubbornly vowed to remember and scribbled a few words on the notepad next to bed before falling into a deep sleep.

Several hours later, I awoke and read the words, **"REMEMBER— THE ANGELS ARE WITH YOU."** I got out of bed knowing two things—my mother would be leaving the Earth and going home very soon, and somehow Archangel Michael and I would find a way to continue on together.

chapter three

Grieve With Reverence

My mother died in her Florida home on Thursday, March 30, 1995. I should not have been surprised; after all, the doctor told her in late December that she had three months to live, and when one of the Hospice nurses asked her in February what day she would die she said Thursday. I thought I was prepared—I knew where she was going and had been informed of the physical changes her body would undergo during the final days and hours of life.

On the Saturday before her passing, she told my sister and me that she had seen the white light, and when we asked her if there was anything else she wanted us to know, she added, "It's all about love." The following Tuesday, she quietly slipped into a coma, and during my evening meditation, I saw my mother sitting on the threshold of the doorway to the Angelic Realm. Yet somewhere deep inside of me, I still refused to believe she would really leave us.

The night Mom died, I was sitting next to her when my feet started hurting. It was just a little discomfort at first, but it soon turned into intense pain, and when Dad got up to go to the bathroom, I moved to his lounge chair to put my feet up. As Dad and I physically separated from her, Mom slipped out of this realm.

My mother's death was so peaceful that it took me completely off guard. Somehow I had created the belief system that dying involved the ripping of the soul out of the body. I had expected a final struggle as my mother took her last breath, perhaps even a shudder as the soul was pulled from the physical body. After my night in the Angelic Realm, I had hoped to see her step into the light, hear something, or at the very least have an awareness that something was going on.

I was even a little angry with my mother for not sharing her crossing with me. So I was not only surprised, I was shocked! However, I reacted the way I always reacted; I denied all of my feelings and simply went numb.

We took Mom back to Illinois for burial, and a few days later, I flew back to Florida to have some time alone before Dad returned. On the flight back, I sat next to a woman who could see I was grieving, and as in the case of many airplane relationships, she listened to my life story. Once I was done she smiled and gently said, "Honey, those pains in your feet were the Angels walking all over you when they came for your mother." I instantly realized that while Mom couldn't share her crossing with me, our Angels had offered me a very physical sign that my life on Earth with Angels was just beginning.

However, before I could begin my new life, I had to let go of my old one. In the past, it had taken a great deal of time and energy to release my old mental, emotional, and physical patterns and behaviors. Luckily, a few weeks after my mother's death, I discovered that the Universe had started this process without me.

The previous January, I had returned to Colorado to close on the sale of my condo and pack up and store my personal belongings. After calling every storage facility in a sixty-mile radius without finding a single vacant unit, a former co-worker offered to store my things in a shed on her land in the mountains. It seemed like a perfect solution at the time. However, after Mom's death, I discovered that my co-worker had filed for divorce and disappeared along with all of my treasures, and I was left with only my car and two suitcases of clothes.

After experiencing a week of some rather intense anger, guilt, and fear over losing the necessities of life in America and the mementos of my past, I relaxed into the freedom of literally not having to deal with my physical baggage. I decided to stay in Florida and easily found a job and an apartment. With some of the money I received from Mom's estate, I began the process of creating a new life from scratch. My first lesson about creating a life of love came quickly; buy only things that you truly love!

My emotional baggage was a little more problematic. By the middle of the summer, I found myself in the throes of menopause at the ripe old age of forty-four. Between the denial of my grief and the hot flashes, headaches, and forgetfulness, I found myself unable to connect with my Angels. No amount of medication or meditation seemed to help, or if it did I quickly forgot. Throughout the fall season I remained in turmoil.

My mother and I had created a wonderful new relationship in the last few months of her life, but I still had not dealt with the pain of our prior relationship. So one afternoon in early November, I went into meditation and asked her to come in. I had not felt her presence or seen any sign that she was trying to contact me, but on that day she was immediately there. I could not only feel her, I could see her as she had been before the cancer ravaged her body.

When she first appeared in my apartment, she seemed confused about where we were, and I gently explained this was my new home. Then I did what I had always wanted to do; I unleashed on my mother. I told her in no uncertain terms what I thought about the way she raised me, including every little detail of how she had wronged me, how she had ignored me, how she loved my brother and sister more than she loved me, how bad she had made me feel all my life, and how angry I was that not only did she die but she didn't let me go into the Angelic Realm with her! The depth and intensity of my desperation, anger, and rage surprised even me, and after about five minutes, I felt both drained and strangely serene.

My mother waited a few seconds, apparently to see if I was really done, then simply said, *"It's a done deal kid, get over it,"* and then she was gone. I actually found that statement rather comforting—it was so Mom.

By Thanksgiving weekend, I still had not been able to connect with the Angels and my yearning had grown so strong that I finally demanded to be allowed into the Angelic Realm. Suddenly, I felt a sharp pain in my right temple as my energy was forcefully ripped from my body. I melted into the oneness and instantly felt the pure love that I had almost forgotten.

I tried to relax into it, but could not. My consciousness seemed paralyzed and just as suddenly as I had been pulled out of my body, I was slammed back into it. My head hurt and when I opened my eyes nothing appeared solid. I could feel things with my hands and feet and move my body around, but I could not see where the wall ended and the couch began.

I soon discovered that I had no sense of balance or taste, and my sense of hearing was distorted, as if I were hearing sounds underwater. As my body slowly returned to normal over the next two days, I had time to reflect on Michael's statement that the vibratory frequency of the Angelic Realm can alter the human body.

While Thanksgiving weekend made me more cautious, it did nothing to dampen my desire to share my life with Angels. As is always the case, the Divine had provided me with exactly what I needed when I needed it. My job had come with two wonderful women, Donna Philp and Deanna Tackett, and the blessings of having these women in my life during this period are beyond explanation. Donna and Deanna put up with my menopausal insanity, helped me to express my grief, shared their lives with me, and eventually coaxed me into laughing again. They were the Earth Angels that sustained and healed me after Mom died.

Shortly before the anniversary of my mother's death, I was in my favorite health food store when I saw a flyer for a weekend seminar with Pat Rodegast channeling Emmanuel. My first encounter with the metaphysical community had occurred nine years earlier when a friend invited me to an Emmanuel reading at a church in Denver. It had been an amazing experience!

Emmanuel was so soft and gentle, not at all like the harshness of my first Michael reading, so I signed up. The first night was a session where Emmanuel answered individual questions. Even though I was terrified of hearing the truth, I found the courage to ask Emmanuel if the experience I had in the Angelic Realm was real or if it had just been a dream.

He quietly said, *"You know it was real, to have such a connection once in a lifetime is a blessing; to experience it more than once is a miracle."*

I went home that night and connected with Archangel Michael for the first time since my mother had died. Michael gently wrapped his energy around me, and instantly my consciousness melted into the oneness of the Angelic Realm. We were greeted by a flurry of dancing energy that felt like a great celebration. *"Little One, a soul is coming home from Earth!"* As the soul fully entered the Angelic Realm, it began to rapidly expand and move outward into infinity.

Even from my protected place within Michael's energy, I could feel the oneness of the realm begin to increase in size, intensity, and movement. As I watched this colorful soul, it became apparent that its expansion was both focused and directed towards those strands it wanted to connect with first. Soon it was literally flying all over the Angelic Realm. Michael let me briefly touch it and I felt what we humans could only call bliss.

I was then drawn to another area of the Angelic Realm where a strand of energy was completely surrounded by a group of other strands, and I realized this energy was an individual soul that had crossed over without melting into the oneness. Michael explained, *"Most souls review their lives in the veil* (white light) *between the physical realm and the Angelic Realm and shed the energy of fear, disease, and other illusions there. However, there are times when the soul chooses to enter the Angelic Realm with lower energy still attached to them. When this occurs, a pocket of love is created for the soul to complete its transformation."*

I asked Michael what causes this and he said there are a lot of reasons. *"Sometimes souls die so suddenly that they do not have time to release all the mental and emotional vibrations from their strand as they leave the physical body. In essence, their Earthly emotional and mental energy doesn't know the body has died. This can occur as the result of an accidental death or some type of violence.*

"Other souls may have died in large groups such as natural disasters, pandemics, or even manmade catastrophes and are looking for another soul that has already crossed over such as a child, parent, or partner. Whatever the reason, no soul is ever left alone; those strands that have assisted the soul on Earth will continue to assist them until they merge back into oneness."

Michael refers to this process as being sequestered and says it's an option for every soul. *"It is the soul that chooses how to experience its transformation. Sometimes the choice to create an experience of being sequestered is made before the soul starts its incarnation, but it can also be made within the lifetime or even at the moment of death. Regardless of how the soul melts back into the oneness, there is always a great celebration."*

I asked Michael if these sequestered souls are in fear and he responded, *"No, it's not possible to remain in fear when there is only pure love surrounding you. A soul's vibratory frequency always rises to meet love. The process of transformation is joyful and all souls want to complete every aspect of the transformation in both the realm they leave and in the realm to which they return.*

"Perhaps you can remember an excess of joy or a flurry of activity in the final days, weeks, and months of your loved one's life. There are final memories to be made and gifts to be both given and received. We can assure you that nothing is left undone. Whether

or not an individual on Earth is consciously aware of the upcoming transformation doesn't really matter. There are no rules or limitations to death."

After watching the celebration of coming home in the Angelic Realm, Michael had me look at death from the Earth's point of view. While the soul was joyously expanding into the Angelic Realm, a hole was appearing in the energy of the physical plane. To pull out a strand of energy leaves a gap in the very fiber of our physical existence.

As I looked at this gap, I felt the intensity of the loss of my own mother and it broke my heart. I knew that once this energy was gone it could never return in the same form. In my pain, I asked Michael what to do when this happens.

Michael's answer was soft and tender. He said, *"Grieve with Reverence. Grieving is a sacred act that says to the soul, 'you are still loved.' The grief, sorrow, and anger a human feels at the death of a loved one whether it is a human, animal, plant, or any other piece of your physical planet is one of the greatest expressions of love mankind has to offer. Grieving with Reverence requires you to feel every emotion as it presents itself.*

"Be gentle with yourself and we assure you that as you honor those you have lost through the full expression of each emotion, you will soon reconnect with loved ones on the other side of the veil. We are aware that our bliss results in your pain. Little one, ask and we will create a safe place in your heart in which you can heal your wounds."

Still feeling the glow of Michael's energy, I returned to my physical body and silently asked the Angels to help me heal the loss of my mother. Immediately, I felt an opening in my heart and embraced the first waves of grief, anger, and sorrow as they began to flow from deep within me.

chapter four

The Gatekeeper

In the spirit of full disclosure, I must tell you that Michael and I disagree to this very day about when I started channeling him. Michael says it was in 1992, and I say it was in 1995. Now I have learned from experience that Angels are always right, but I also realize that humans must take responsibility for their own lives and assert their free will and belief systems, even when they know there is a possibility they are wrong. I have done this all my life, well at least since I was two, because I like to be right.

Michael seems somewhat amused by this approach to life on Earth, and is wise enough to realize that under these circumstances, my lessons on Earth require a lot more assistance than he alone can give.

My lessons about channeling have come from many wonderful people, animals, plants, crystals, rocks, rivers, and even mountains that I have met on my journey. I was blessed with the opportunity to have several private sessions with Pat Rodegast and Emmanuel that validated the information I was receiving from Michael, and taught me how to embrace my new reality. I also met many other compassionate energy healers who offered me tools that helped me cope with the physical changes of menopause and the mental upheavals that my grief brought to the surface.

However, it was the dolphins at Theater of the Sea in Key Largo that reached inside me and touched my mind and emotions. When I would swim with them, I could feel their sonar tickling the inside of my body. I had kidney surgery as a child and in the process my right kidney was pulled up and attached to my fifth rib muscle. The dolphins seemed fascinated by my unsymmetrical kidneys. Time after time, they gently approached me and caressed my back with their beaks. This physical connection made me feel so special that the years of embarrassment over my eleven-inch surgical scar dissolved away during our first swim.

The bottle-nosed dolphins that I swam with weighed up to five hundred pounds and were almost six feet in length, yet I felt totally safe with them. As they moved through the water, I watched them dodge in and out of each other's paths and could almost sense their total awareness of each other. Their great speed, agility and flexibility reminded me of the Angelic Realm as each individual animal moved in perfect synchronicity with all others and the pod seemed to merge into one entity.

I still find myself feeling jealous of the movements of dolphins as they fly through the water as easily as the Angels fly through the Angelic Realm. In comparison, I feel like a land locked klutz!

The experience of swimming with dolphins always touches a primal love that exists deep within me. Dolphins are so curious, gentle, and playful that I immediately return to the awe and wonder that I knew as a child at the mere sight of one. Luckily, after the second or third time that I swam with them, they started coming into my dreams and meditations. I seem to be able to breathe underwater quite easily in my sleep and always understand exactly what they are saying to me. I have been able to accept a kinship with the dolphins that has always eluded me with humans. For this blessing I am infinitely grateful.

My time in Florida changed me in ways that I will never understand. Prior to my visits into the Angelic Realm, I had always experienced the sensation of leaving my body when connecting with Michael and other higher energies. This limited my contact with Spirit to my deep meditations and sessions when I channeled for others. While I loved this feeling, it often left me unfulfilled and longing for more. So in his infinite wisdom, Michael began to present me with options that would allow me to feel his presence whenever I asked.

Michael's most interesting offer was to serve as my gatekeeper. Every time I heard the word gatekeeper, I envisioned being in my perfect little cottage surrounded by a white picket fence with Michael standing at the front gate checking the IDs of everyone who came along—allowing my friends in while turning away solicitors, debt collectors, and dark entities.

I had known for years that when people energetically opened up to other realms and higher vibratory frequencies, they also opened up to lower energies. I had vivid memories of feeling very frightened, angry, and even physically ill for days at a time without the slightest idea that these feelings were being caused by an entity that had attached to me. I really just wanted to be freed from this type of intrusion.

However, Michael had a more expanded view of gatekeepers. While he assured me that as my gatekeeper he would indeed make decisions about which energies would be allowed into my physical being and auric field, his primary purpose would be to hold my personal doorway and connection to the Angelic Realm wide open at all times.

He told me, *"Little One, there will be moments when your human mind will try to protect you from pain by blocking your knowledge of the Divine, and your emotions will ask you to seek comfort in the forgetting of your planet. However, when you are focused on and connected to the Divine Love of your eternal soul, no life consciousness on Earth can intrude into your energy or harm you in any way. A gatekeeper protects you by continuously reminding you of your Angelic/human connection, surrounding you with your own Divine Love, and melting into oneness with you on the Earth plane."*

Immediately upon accepting Michael as my gatekeeper, he became permanently positioned in my energy field, and I began to physically feel his presence next to me. I felt totally protected. Once my fear of being intruded upon was eliminated, I was able to read or "feel" the energy coming through me in its purest form. Angelic, psychic, fairy, underworld, and all types of information flow on the vibratory frequencies of their source, and Michael immediately began teaching me how to read and interpret these energy flows.

At times, I still received fear-based information; I just knew it was fear-based. That is, unless I had been drinking! Alcohol seems to inhibit my ability to discern vibratory frequencies, so if you ever meet me in a bar or at a wedding, I suggest you refrain from asking me to connect you with Michael. In that moment, I will be absolutely certain I am talking to him, but chances are I am really talking to an alcohol-crazed entity.

While I loved the people around me and loved swimming with dolphins, the heat and humidity of Florida drained me physically, and my rent and other expenses were increasing at twice the rate of my salary. My father had remarried and was very happy, so I decided it was time to move on and began asking for guidance about where to go next.

I missed the Colorado Rockies, but was worried that I could no longer handle the cold winters. Then on vacation in the Smoky Mountains, I discovered the small town of Waynesville, North Carolina. My first day there, I went to McDonalds for lunch where a preschooler ran up to me and said, "Look Mom, it's the Angel Lady!" His mother told him that was nice, and then told me that he had been talking about the Angel Lady for the past two months.

Several months later, I moved to Waynesville, found several part-time jobs, and even made my first attempt at self-employment through channeling. It was the first time that I had openly admitted to a community that I talked to Angels, and while it was all very exciting, it was totally unsuccessful.

I found that people either loved the idea of working with Angels or were completely offended by it. I also found that many people who wanted Angelic information placed no value on the time and effort it took for me to retrieve it. It did not take long for me to learn that I needed to be selective about who I talked to about my work.

Fortunately, I met a wonderful Celtic Shaman who taught me, among other things, that fairies like chocolate. I spent many summer afternoons sitting under my favorite tree, studying Celtic belief systems, rituals, and traditions while talking to the local fairies and eating chocolate.

As I opened my mind to forgotten memories of my soul, the fairies and the female essence of the Smoky Mountains wrapped me in their healing energy and I became healthy and strong once again. I began to enjoy the freedom of menopause as my body found a new balance. I left my youth behind and embraced the mature woman I was becoming as I surrendered to the fullness of my true self.

Then on a warm August afternoon as I was hiking in the mountains, I sat down at the base of a waterfall to rest for a few minutes. I closed my eyes and took a few deep breaths and within moments was back in the Angelic Realm with Michael.

As I began to fly across the realm, I became aware that my consciousness was actively seeking out the strands that I knew as the fairies, mountains, rocks, water, plants, and animals of the area that was physically surrounding me on Earth. I was in oneness with the natural world of my planet!

On this visit, I asked no questions and was simply told, *"The time to move on is near."* Amidst the pure love of the Angelic Realm and my own planet, I could feel Emmanuel's truth inside of me, *"To have such a connection once in a lifetime is a blessing; to experience it more than once is a miracle."* This miracle was about learning to just BE, and I accepted this gift with a joy that I had not known I was capable of feeling.

chapter five

The Spiritual Dance Of Earth

I have a habit of making my life more difficult than it needs to be, and the decision about my next move was no exception. I longed to live somewhere where I would feel in complete oneness with humanity and the Earth. My earliest childhood memories included the beliefs that I was adopted and that I had mistakenly arrived on the wrong planet at the wrong time. I still occasionally think I'm adopted, but I let go of the wrong planet idea in 1980 when I moved to Colorado and suddenly felt like I was coming home for the first time.

So of course my first thought was of returning to the majestic mountains that I had known for almost fifteen years of my life. Yet something was holding me back, and the more I tried to mediate the split between my mind and emotions, the more confused I became.

Looking back, I now know that this struggle was about self-love. However, at the time, I was just a human being that had experienced a difficult year in which everything I tried seemed to fail. I had been unable to make a living working in traditional settings, and the one thing that I loved doing most in the world, channeling Michael, seemed to be of little value in the marketplace of my planet.

The duality of my life was overwhelming. I had experienced not just one, but three Divine connections in the Angelic Realm. I felt like the most blessed person on the Earth and knew that even one moment in the Angelic Realm was enough to sustain a lifetime. I was truly humbled and very angry! My logic dictated that if one could experience the oneness and unconditional love of the Angelic Realm, one should also be able to create a life of financial abundance and bliss on Earth.

The fact that I was having difficulty connecting to others and financially surviving had to be my fault. There had to be a character flaw or some darkness within me that prevented the colors of the Angelic Realm from flowing through me. Colorado was my heaven on Earth, and I was not yet worthy of admittance.

Once the decision of where not to move was made, I surrendered and asked for my next step. While Spirit is non-intrusive, once invited in, it is very efficient. In less than a week, three people approached me with stories about Flagstaff, Arizona. I had never heard of this town so I asked Michael to show me if these messages were from him, and that night there was a story on television about Flagstaff, and then two more within the next three days.

I was convinced and my mind and emotions immediately relaxed as a sense of peace returned to my daily life. Moving halfway across the country to a place that I had never been before was not a problem for me; I had done it when I moved to Colorado. I packed up the car and headed west. I must admit that when I got to Albuquerque, New Mexico, there was a pull on my heart to turn north onto I-25 towards Colorado, but I was in the left-hand lane during rush hour traffic and just kept going.

Once I got to Flagstaff, I quickly found an apartment and a job as a Juvenile Probation Officer. I have a Master's Degree in Child Development and Family Studies and much prefer working in early childhood enrichment and prevention programs, but I have found throughout my career that programs that deal with fixing and controlling behavior problems pay better. In my younger years, this type of work suited my personality and belief systems; however, my increasing connection to Spirit was making this more difficult for me. Fixing and controlling others was beginning to feel more like fear and less like love.

I also began channeling part-time and joined a weekly Reiki (hands on healing) group where I met some wonderful people, including Suzanne Pittman. When Suz first touched me with her Reiki energy, I felt like I was back in the Angelic Realm. Her energy was so soft and when it merged with the healing energy of Reiki, all my fears just melted away and I felt whole.

After a year of personal solitude, it was wonderful to find a new friend, and we even discovered that we had both recently moved to Flagstaff from Waynesville, North Carolina. Even with this glaring coincidence staring me in the face, I had no idea how important this relationship would be to my Divine Path in the future!

Another life changing event occurred soon after I arrived in Arizona. I was dropping off a donation at the Humane Society when I made the fatal error of seeing the puppies out of the corner of my eye. I had no intention of getting a dog, but a five-pound ball of white and brown fluff had a different idea. This little critter started crying and whimpering so pathetically that I had no choice but to pick it up and comfort it. My apartment complex allowed dogs up to thirty pounds and the puppy was listed as an Aussie mix with as estimated adult weight of twenty to twenty-five pounds. After a heart wrenching seven minutes, I gave in and took the puppy home.

I was so enamoured with this creature that I didn't even notice he was a male until later that night, and since I had always had female dogs there were a number of surprises ahead. The first was his name. I tried at least fifteen wonderfully original and exclusive names and he would not respond to any of them, so I finally gave up and just started calling him Buddy.

This was a puppy who knew who he was, and within a few weeks, he opened up my life to the world of dog parks, doggie day care, and dog people. Our weekends were filled with Saturday mornings at the park and afternoon hikes in the forests of the White Mountains. I was feeling both fulfilled and connected in my new home, and I was absolutely positively sure that Michael had sent Buddy to me!

Even though I was feeling very fulfilled in my outer life, I was aware of a gnawing feeling deep inside of me that all was not exactly as it should be. My professional life and various aspects of my personal life were literally split in two. The interests that I shared with one group were dismissed and often scorned by members of the other groups.

Up until this point in my life, this had been very normal for me. I had a lot of different interests and was able to easily take on different roles for different people. In other words, I was able to listen, read people, and think, say, and do what they expected of me. I was truly artful at being conditioned by the world around me. The problem was that I never let people see and get to know the real me, at least not all of me. So if they didn't like me I was comforted by the fact that they did not know me, but if they did like me I was disappointed in the knowledge that what they liked was really just an illusion.

Archangel Michael was different. This spiritual being knew everything about me; nothing can be hidden from an Angel. Yet with all of this knowledge, Michael still loved all of me. I could feel Michael loving my darkness, my shadows, and everything else that I hated about myself. I was grateful for this love; it filled me up and gave me the courage I needed to get through the great suffering and the bad hair days of my life, but it also confused and irritated me.

How could I ever figure out who I was "supposed to BE" and become truly worthy and spiritual if Michael refused to condemn, or at least point out, the bad in me? Finally, I just asked, "What is spirituality?"

This question marked a subtle change in our relationship. Prior to this, I communicated with Michael only when I was doing things that I believed were spiritual such as meditation, hands-on healing, channeling, and prayer. While I felt his presence around me at other times, I had always assumed that Michael's love was so great that he loved me in spite of my darkness. Now I was beginning to understand that Michael really loved all the darkness and fear of Earth. This confused me even more, "How can fear and love both be worthy of Divine Love?"

Archangel Michael used my job as a Probation Officer to make his point. During meditation, Michael would ask me to look at the energy of each child I worked with. Surprisingly, he always asked me to look at the dark energy in each child first and then look for the light.

Over the next few months, I discovered three things. First, I must say that the light is easier to find in the dark. It's like taking a flashlight out into the bright sunlight, even if you hold it up to your eyes it's often hard to tell if the light is on or off. However, if you take that flashlight into a dark closet and turn it on, the light is blinding. It was the same with these kids. Many of them had been abused and neglected, were failing in school, and felt as if no one in the world loved them. Yet each of them showed intense moments of love and compassion for others, found joy and laughter in the most unusual of circumstances, and continued to believe that things would change. The light flourished within them.

The next thing that I noticed was that the contrast of the light and dark is incredibly beautiful, and to remove one or the other would leave a dull and boring existence behind. Michael began to explain to me that the Divine Plan of Earth includes the duality of love and fear and reminded me of a Taoist saying, "To know what love is, is to know what love is not."

"Your Divine Plan on Earth includes both knowing and expressing fear. You have come here to learn about fear, and the use of fear to control, manipulate, and demean each other is an energy pattern of your planet. Each life consciousness of Earth must learn about fear in order to discern the difference between love and fear."

This statement broke my heart—everything in me told me that my journey on Earth is about love. How can this be? Michael then asked me to back up, and as I did I suddenly saw and understood the wider picture. Whether we are in the Angelic Realm or here on Earth, it is very easy to love when everyone and everything around us is pure love, but it's not so easy to love when one is surrounded by fear and darkness.

However, when an individual chooses to love within darkness, a completely new hue or tint of color is added to its original strand, giving it added richness and depth. To love through the darkness of fear creates a love that has never existed before, even in the Angelic Realm. This new love expands not only the individual expressing it, but the Earth and Angelic Realm as well. The experience of fear is spiritual, not because of its expression, but because it offers us the choice to create new forms of love. We must enter and express fear in order to choose love, and no matter how painful it seems, love and fear are partners in the spiritual dance of Earth.

The last thing I discovered was about me. It is much easier for me to accept the darkness in others than to accept that same darkness in myself, and my instinct is to look for the light in others while obsessing over my own flaws. Unfortunately, this process of selective seeing has prevented me from grasping the full meaning, excitement, and beauty of life on Earth.

Spirituality is the wholeness of the dark and light within our lives, the sadness and the happiness, the grief and the joy, the anger and the forgiveness, the war and the peace, the fear and the love. There is not one moment lost in our pain and suffering, for all the darkness within us merely serves as the backdrop through which the light streams out of the portrait of our lives.

Still, as a human I am acutely aware that it is very difficult to believe that darkness has a purpose in the moment we are experiencing it. I think true faith includes the hope that the terrible darkness in our lives will one day reveal the beauty of its purpose.

I must admit that being told that my darkness is as spiritual as my light released the pressure cooker boiling inside of me. Knowing that imperfection is spiritual perfection allowed me to begin to relax into myself for the first time in my life.

chapter six

How Do We Get Here?

When I was in elementary school, my parents took me to the Museum of Natural Science and Industry in Chicago. It was a magical place with bi-planes attached to the ceiling, a submarine that you could walk into, a mine that you could ride through on a tram, and all sorts of mechanical, electrical, sound, light, outer space, and ocean exhibits. I loved science, but my favorite exhibit was a dollhouse.

This dollhouse had belonged to some European princess. It was huge and fully equipped with electric lights, a swimming pool, a real kitchen, and room after room of the most beautiful furniture, draperies, and art anyone could imagine. Even the food on the table and the flowers in the garden appeared to be fresh and alive. There was a ramp that allowed you to walk all the way around the exhibit but kept you far enough away that you could not touch it.

From the first moment I saw this wondrous mansion, I knew that if I focused hard enough I could place my consciousness inside of this house and live there for the rest of my life. I was pretty sure that I was adopted, so this move seemed natural for me—this was the luxurious home that I was supposed to be living in.

I concentrated very hard, and just as I began to feel myself in my new bedroom, a very rude person nudged me forward in line, jerking me back into my body, and leaving me convinced that if I had been given a few more minutes, I would be living like a princess today.

Almost forty years later, I would witness another similar experience, only this time in the Angelic Realm. It happened spontaneously on a very hot Sunday afternoon in September of 1999. My dog, Buddy, and I were hiking in the forest when I sat down to rest and eat a chocolate bar. We had not seen any other people for over an hour so I closed my eyes and began listening to the birds.

In seconds, I was back in the Angelic Realm with Michael at my side. I was excited; it had been over two years since my last visit. I began to fly through my energy strand and melt into old friends. Then Michael gently brought my focus back to him and said, *"You asked me how you get to Earth, let me show you."*

Before we go any further, I would like to stop and say that Michael said this with the energy of pure innocence, as if I had just asked the question a moment ago. For the human Viki, it had been four years since I had asked that question. I'm pointing this out not to complain about being offered this information—this is an extraordinary question and I was thrilled to be getting the answer. I'm merely trying to show other humans what it is like to communicate with Angels that live outside of time.

As an impatient human, I have always prayed and looked for the answer to come in the next moment, hour, day, or week. After that, I usually quit looking, believing I must be unworthy of receiving what I asked for. In the fall of 1999, I was just beginning to understand that every prayer is heard and answered whether we humans realize it or not. This is true for everyone on Earth, but I would not put it past Michael to try and teach me a little patience through his casual approach to answering a question posed so long ago!

I must admit that the realization that four years had passed did not come until after I returned to my body. When I am in the Angelic Realm, I am like Michael, outside of time, so in that moment the question and the answer seemed to gently flow through me without missing a beat.

Michael began his answer by guiding me to an individualized strand of energy. This soul was surrounded by a large number of other strands that were melting in and out of it at different points along its surface. Each time a different strand melted into the individual, the hue or tint of color changed in that spot. As this process proceeded, the color of the soul seemed to grow in length, width, and depth and its energy began to vary in speed as it created forms and geometrical shapes within its being. It was mesmerizing to watch, and at one point I felt myself join the process as I merged with the strand.

As I was pulled back from the encounter, I asked Michael what was happening. He explained, *"This strand is about to enter the Earth plane and all of the strands surrounding it, including yours, are helping it prepare for the journey ahead. The human Viki will meet this soul in human form in Earth's future time, which is why you touched it.*

"Some of the strands that surround the soul are in physical form on the Earth. The parents, siblings, relatives, and future friends, are all involved in the process. Additional strands will assist the individual from the Angelic Realm as Guardian and other Angels, and still others are incarnate on other planets in the physical universe and in other realms.

"Every incarnation is well planned out; however, like all journeys, once it begins there are many surprises along the way. In fact, it is the unexpected moments that bring the greatest joy and expansion to every experience. The mysteries of life draw the soul back, over and over again, to experience life from different perspectives. All souls are very curious!"

Michael then directed me to the area in the Angelic Realm that I had previously recognized as Earth. I again observed that the energy of this area appeared to be contained within a boundary and was moving slower than that of the surrounding Angelic Realm. As I was watching the energy of Earth, I became aware of the slowing of the energy within the strand preparing for incarnation. I could sense the soul moving into synchronicity with the energy of the physical realm, and then it began to pulsate. This was a new experience for me and it was very exciting!

Suddenly, I felt an expansion of the energy around me that seemed to create a wave that moved across the Angelic Realm toward the strand. As if the soul could sense the wave coming, it began to shape itself into a rotating spiral. As the wave reached the strand, it was picked up and carried towards the physical realm, and as the outer edge of the spiral pierced the boundary, the soul entered the Earth plane and the wave dissipated. I could feel a glow of light rise from the entry point and hear the echoes of a new song coming from my planet.

Finally, the pulsation of the strand's energy that remained in the Angelic Realm began to slow until it melted softly back into the oneness of its support system. Michael did not have to say a thing; I already knew that somewhere on Earth a baby had just been conceived.

I gently returned to my physical body and was greeted by sloppy wet dog kisses. Buddy seems to enjoy this behavior and has been known to lick children for up to ten minutes (he would have gone longer, but the kids couldn't stand it anymore). I liked it when he was a puppy and had dry little kisses, but my little Aussie had grown into a fifty-pound dog that could lick you raw in under three minutes. Based on the condition of my face, he had been at it for quite some time.

However, it did serve to bring me back to Earth, and as I began to once again walk in my physical world, the colors of the sky and forest appeared to take on a new life and depth as the steady rhythm of crunching pine needles beneath my feet accompanied the vibrant songs of the birds. The symphony of life was putting on a performance, and for the first time in many years, I was choosing to be a part of it.

The changes that occurred within me following this trip into the Angelic Realm were both subtle and far-reaching. The sensation of taking part in my own life continues to this day, and that feeling of being adopted and never quite belonging has disappeared. Witnessing how we come to Earth taught me that there are no accidents.

We choose to come to Earth—we plan it, we are excited about it, and even though we come as a single soul in a separate body, we are still in the oneness of the Angelic Realm.

This inner shift began a series of changes in my outer world as well. I left my job with the Juvenile Court and began teaching classes on connecting with Angels in addition to channeling. I also discovered that my channeling was changing as I became more aware of what my clients were saying and feeling. I began to realize that all the wonderful love that I was feeling in my body as I channeled Michael was not being felt by those I was reading for.

I asked Michael if there was a way that I could help people feel the Angelic energy that I was feeling and he explained, *"Humans feel Angelic energy (love) as it flows through their bodies. However, physical bodies must be at a vibratory frequency that is high enough to sustain the flow of Angelic energy, or it can physically harm them. Our readings are designed to assist them in raising their frequency to that level."*

So I asked Michael if there was a way that we could create a pocket of Angelic energy that people could sit in and feel on their skin. He replied, *"We'll work on it."*

As had been the case for years, my channeling and classes were not enough to financially support me, so I began looking for another job and found a position with the Health Start Program. This was a state program that provided services for pregnant women in our area. Anyone was eligible for the program, but we focused on the Navajo reservation, teenagers, and the local Spanish-speaking population.

We hired and trained individuals that lived in these communities to provide whatever was needed such as food, prenatal care, emotional support, education, and transportation to assure the delivery of healthy babies. This program changed the way I live my life.

The Navajo people are amazing. There is a great deal of poverty on the reservation with few job opportunities or even modern facilities, yet it is a striking environment where time flows in the current of the natural world. The Navajo people are connected to Mother Earth and to each other in a way that I had only previously experienced in the Angelic Realm. I am forever humbled and grateful to them for accepting and teaching me about themselves and their rituals.

I learned how to quietly express BEING on Earth from many of the Navajo staff and women that I came to know. I felt safe with them because I knew that they understood what it was like to be living a seemingly mundane life of struggle and survival while simultaneously connecting to something so much greater than ourselves that it fills our lives with an eternal wonder and awe. The duality of Earth became softer and more bearable for me through my connection with their culture.

I learned a great deal about different cultures, ideas and belief systems—and about the common desire to nurture and raise healthy children—from all the women that I met and worked with at Health Start. As I opened to new cultures and let go of many of my preconceived ideas and expectations, I suddenly found babies opening up to me.

After years of communicating only with my Gatekeeper, suddenly hearing other voices in my head was a bit disconcerting. There was also the problem of babies trying to get my attention while I was interviewing their mothers, which was very distracting, so I tried to ignore them at first. I soon learned that babies just prior to conception, and in utero, are very pushy, you might even say bossy!

These souls communicated through a very rapid flow of consciousness that was difficult for me to keep up with. It also lacked emotion, which made it hard for me to understand the context in which they were communicating. After the first few weeks, I begged Michael for a little help in dealing with this rampant invasion of my head.

As usual, Michael knew exactly what was happening and what to do. He explained that when I touched the incarnating soul during my last visit to the Angelic Realm, I connected as both a soul of the Angelic Realm and as a human of Earth. The energy of this joining rippled across the Angelic Realm allowing incoming souls to communicate with me.

As close as I can tell, I seem to have acquired the language used by every incarnating human baby on the planet. However, while I seem to understand the language, I cannot speak it. The new souls don't seem to realize I cannot speak to them and when I don't answer them, they just assume I will do what they ask. This makes them seem bossier than they really are.

Most of the time, the babies wanted their mothers to eat protein, take vitamins, drink more milk, lay off the caffeine, play certain music, exercise, rest more, stop fighting with dad, and at times they even offered preferences for their birth plans and I was able to deliver the majority of this information easily.

I grew to love these connections and at times had more personal conversations with the babies. The first time this occurred, I was working with a young girl, pregnant by incest, and trying to decide whether or not to have the baby. I was sitting quietly as the counselor talked with the mother when the baby's consciousness came in so loudly that I could no longer hear the voices around me.

The baby chastised me for thinking that this was a horrible situation. It then told me. *"Whenever a call for love is made, it is answered. My mother opened her heart in a terrible moment of darkness and fear and asked to be loved. I openly and joyfully answered, 'YES, I WILL LOVE YOU.' I came to Earth in love and if it is most loving for me to stay, I will stay. If it becomes more loving for me to leave, I will leave."*

On another occasion I sat with a mother as she lost the baby she had so desperately wanted. As the human life was slipping away the baby asked me to stay and grieve with her mother and then said, *"Tell her thank you for being my mom. My life is complete; I have known only the pure love of her heart, and it was more than I ever imagined Earth could be."*

I later asked Michael if all babies that leave before birth feel that way and he said, *"Every one of them."*

chapter seven

The True Essence Of Love

When a baby is born, it has as many active neurons in its brain as there are stars in the Milky Way Galaxy. My Health Start staff and I were given the opportunity to take Doula training and assist many of our mothers in childbirth.

An amazing thing happens at birth. As the head emerges from the mother, the baby automatically turns to allow its shoulders to slide out and then opens its eyes to view the light of our world for the first time. I always positioned myself so that I could look into its eyes at that moment, and every time it took my breath away. It was like looking into the very center of our galaxy. The depth of those eyes, and the light that seemed to literally pour out of them, still remains one of the greatest mysteries of life.

Intuitively, I knew that I was looking into the soul of that baby and perhaps even seeing a glimpse of the realm from which it came. However, as a human I was witnessing the very creation of our physical realm expanding right in front of me.

But the magic did not stop there! While I was unable to connect with the newborn's flow of consciousness, I could connect with its energy, and quickly learned that we humans are very interesting at birth. We are still connected to the Angels and other realms, even as we begin to create new relationship on Earth. We continue to talk to both Angels and humans in the language of Spirit for many months after birth. Infants, even those that are blind, can see the auras or spiritual energy of those around them long before they begin to recognize human faces. They also know how we are all connected in the Angelic Realm, and understand our individual Divine Paths on Earth.

These tiny creatures are very wise, and simply touching them physically or energetically can remind the rest of us who we really are and why we are here. However, all humans agree to forget this information upon our arrival in the physical world, and while it takes years to forget everything, our infants embrace and become human very quickly.

The Health Start program assisted families through the first two years of the child's life. As I watched the infants lovingly let go of their identities as Spirits, I learned how humans forget who they really are. This knowledge allowed me to travel backwards in my own forgetting, expanding into the memory and knowledge of my own unique Divine Purpose.

Surprisingly, my first reaction to this remembering was emotional. It seemed that Michael had been encouraging me to express my emotions for quite some time, but I had not been listening. Hopefully the babies would be more successful!

Slowly, my journey back in time began to reveal the roots of my repressed emotions. My family frowned on negative behaviors and emotions, yet by the time I was three, I was an expert at crying and whining. These behaviors were the expressions of both the physical pain of my kidney disease and the anger, sadness, grief, and other fears this pain ignited within me.

My mother, who was unaware of my kidney problems, did not like these behaviors and taught me they were unacceptable. Being the dutiful child that I was, I learned to deny my emotions along with these behaviors. I also learned (and I have no idea where or how I learned this) that I should not be happy until everyone around me was happy. We lived in a small town with a large extended family in which someone was always upset, so I found very little opportunity to express happiness and soon began to ignore this emotion as well.

The older I got, the more emotions I chose to bury inside of me. There were occasions when a boatload of emotions would suddenly explode from within me, but they were few and far between. My numbness helped me to survive the pain and darkness of my physical life for many years.

Unconsciously, I also believed that my joy and happiness had to be hidden deep inside of me to protect it from the negativity of the Earth and my own humanity. It was as if I was trying to save the positive side of myself from the dark side of myself. I truly believed that the darkness within me was larger and more powerful than any light. Fortunately, as the babies helped me to remember the immensity of my own light, I also remembered the loving power of my emotions and realized that I had never learned how to express them.

Michael responded to this realization. *"Little One, you are an emotional empath. You literally feel the emotions of others in your body. As a child, the emotions of others overpowered you and left you unable to feel your own emotions. You did not learn how to express your own emotions because you were too busy trying to learn how to manage the emotions of others.*

"Your human mind could not understand what was happening and taught you to focus on your thoughts in order to survive. It was a necessary and loving thing to do. Your mind was protecting you by allowing you to think, rather than feel, your way through the world. But it has been a great burden for your mind and has brought you great stress and sadness. It is time to let go of your empathic ability for a while and begin to explore and learn how to express all that you feel in each moment." I agreed, and together Michael and I shut down my empathic skills.

Immediately, there was a rather frightening sense of silence within me. I was aware of the noise created by my thoughts, but I had no idea that emotions could be so loud. In comparison to thoughts, the sounds of emotions are muffled and deeper in tone, much like hearing underwater. I could feel the current of the emotional sound flowing through me, but at first, I had difficulty sorting out the individual emotions in my body.

In the past, I would often feel happy when someone else was angry, and I had learned that I needed to be angry to be happy. As I felt grief and sadness while those around me experienced the pride of accomplishment, I discovered that my own success in life seemed to be accompanied by disappointment and despair. I was an adult with a child's grasp of emotions. Once my empathic skills were turned off, I was completely lost, and even my mind could not help me.

I soon discovered that Spirit had provided me with the perfect teachers for my current situation. While I had spent the last decade learning how to quiet my mind in meditation, the Navajo people had spent hundreds of years perfecting their relationship with silence. The Navajo have a way of resting in the silence, observing all that is going on around them without the need to interfere, to change, or even to take part in the actions of those around them. They have the ability to silently observe!

Once I learned this art, I was able to experience my own feelings for the first time. I felt as if, one by one, my emotions were being presented to me. I had no choice but to feel them in my body, wrap them in my thoughts, and express them to the world. Strangely enough, when I did this my world did not end; in fact, I actually began to enjoy the sensations of my emotions.

As I embraced all that I felt in my body, I found myself categorizing my emotions as positive and negative. My mind was actually very helpful in this process; it taught me that anger, rage, depression, sadness, jealousy, and a host of others were negative while happiness, joy, bliss, generosity, and gratitude were positive. It became very easy for me to divide my life into fear (negative) and love (positive) based on these emotions, and soon I was feeling pleased with myself, perhaps even a bit enlightened!

Michael let me play with my emotions and sense of enlightenment for about a year. Then he took me back into the Angelic Realm. One moment I was in my rocking chair listening to soft Celtic music, and the next moment I was expanding into infinity. This time Michael seemed to expand with me, and then he reached out and touched me.

This was another new experience; we were not melting into one another, yet this touch created an overwhelming flow of blue and white energy that radiated outward through my entire strand! I could not respond, and there seemed to be no reason to even try. I simply let this love fill me with its timelessness.

Eventually, Michael called to my consciousness and I was able to focus on the task at hand. I have been aware since my first trip into the Angelic Realm that our human emotions, like our minds and bodies, are left behind in the physical realm. There does seem to be a sense of curiosity in the oneness, but what I overwhelmingly feel is what we humans would describe as pure love, so I asked Michael to explain what had just happened.

He said, *"There is a great deal of confusion about love on the Earth plane. Most people believe that love is an emotion. However, love is not an emotion. Love is the essence of who you really are. Love is the eternal energy of the God source that creates and flows through all that is. We just touched you with love and what you experienced was the love of God flowing through your infinite being, including your human body.*

"When a life consciousness allows love to flow through the mind, body, and emotions, love is expressed on Earth. When that same life consciousness blocks the flow of love, the result is an expression of fear. There are no positive or negative emotions.

"Your anger is positive when love guides you to protect, nurture,

and take loving actions to help others and create justice out of injustice. That same anger becomes negative when fear offers the choice to place blame, punish, and seek revenge on others. Little One, it is time to let go of the idea of negative and positive emotions and simply let your love flow. It is time to love all of your emotions!"

I was a little startled by the idea that love on Earth is not an emotion. Everything on Earth seems to revolve around the search for love, and then I remembered something that Emmanuel had told me shortly after Mom died, *"You do not need to learn how to love; you need to learn how to express love!"*

Michael continued, *"Little One, every life consciousness on Earth is love. Currently on your planet, humans spend most of their time teaching children and each other how to forget who they are. This is necessary to fully embrace and join humanity. However, love cannot be denied, so humans must create an illusion of love. This illusion is often more about fear than love, but it does sustain you until it is time for each of you to awaken to the true essence of love within you."*

I asked Michael about the concept of following your heart. I followed my head for most of my life and felt unfulfilled. Over the last few years, I had tried following my heart by making a living by doing what I love the most, channeling Michael, and that had not worked either.

Michael gently explained, *"Most individuals that say they are following their hearts are really reacting to their emotions. Reacting to your emotions, your mind, or your gut instincts (body) are all human choices. Expressing your spiritual essence through your humanity is a bit more difficult on Earth. Patience, Little One, you are getting there!"* This last statement seemed to be accompanied by harps; I was back in the physical realm.

This new experience in the Angelic Realm taught me what it feels like to have my spiritual essence flowing through me. I spent the next year practicing with the babies who seemed to recognize and even laugh at my attempts to let Spirit flow.

Then late one afternoon, I was driving home when I saw an elderly woman standing alone beside a rock formation. The clouds were building and I knew a storm was approaching so I pulled over to ask if she wanted a ride. Once I stopped the car, I couldn't see her so I got out and walked toward the rocks.

Suddenly, I saw the image of a female on the face of the rock and heard, *"It's time to return to Colorado. The new children will be looking for you there."* Needless to say there was no woman. It started raining, and a few months later, when the lease on my apartment was up, I moved back to Colorado Springs.

chapter eight

Time To Go Home

They say that you can't go home again, but you can. What's interesting is what happens when you get there. Needless to say, I had changed a great deal over the past eight years, but you would not have known it by my behavior. I immediately began reconnecting with old acquaintances in the holistic community and looking for a traditional mainstream job.

It took me several months to find a job in an Early Intervention Program assisting children with special needs. This greatly strained my finances, but fifteen months later, I was able to purchase a small townhome and set up a home office for my channeling. It appeared that I had reclaimed all that I had given up by moving to Florida!

On the surface, I had my life back. The problem was that I was different and this wonderful life didn't fit anymore. I had spent years working in Social Service agencies guided by rules and regulations and had enjoyed the intellectual approach to designing and delivering services to families. However, no matter how hard I tried, I could no longer repress or deny the spiritual communications I was receiving.

The children would come into my dreams and tell me what they needed, and quite often what they needed and what the agency had to offer were in opposition. In the Health Start program, I would have openly discussed what the children were saying with their parents, therapists, and other team members, but this was not acceptable behavior in my current situation.

Colorado Springs is a very conservative area, and only one or two other staff members had the ability to access this type of information; the rest of the staff did not believe that it was even possible to communicate with the kids in this way. The more I tried to reconcile the information I received from the children with the belief systems of those I worked with, the greater the conflict I created within myself and with those around me.

More importantly, I missed Michael. The hours I spent at work separated us, and our readings had become sporadic. I was still meditating, but even that had gone from a daily to a weekly activity and in each meditation Michael repeated, *"Little One, you must love yourself as you love me."*

This statement further frustrated me. How could I possibly love myself as I loved Michael? Michael was pure love and I was a mess. For months, I ignored Michael's words and continued to try all sorts of holistic rituals and healings in order to balance my path of love and fear, oneness and separation, peace and chaos.

Finally, over Thanksgiving weekend of 2003, Michael pulled me back into the Angelic Realm, and Archangel Uriel was also there to greet me. Uriel and I had a rather strained relationship. For reasons unknown, I had always felt like a helpless child in his presence. I wasn't afraid of him, but the minute I felt his energy, I thought I was in trouble, and this encounter was no exception. Uriel's presence stopped me in my tracks and I did not try to fly across the realm, I simply tried to hide behind Michael's energy, hoping Uriel wouldn't see me.

Of course, when you're in oneness there is no hiding! Luckily, I was not in trouble; in fact it seemed that my little human adventure back into my old habits of fear and conditioning actually amused the Angels. I must say that the experience of being tag-teamed by two Archangels was very interesting. The amount of energy and information that I felt was much greater than that of Michael alone, but the two of them melted into a single consciousness.

They started by having me focus on a section of my own blue strand and asking me to describe its path. That was easy; this was the last thirty years of my adult life, in which I had been consciously setting the intention to be of service to children. The Angels then asked me to back up, and as I did, an aqua blue light began to emerge out of the consciousness of this section of my strand. As I felt these two very different shades of blue, I understood that my life on Earth was about to change. I could feel this new energy and longed to flow into it and create it on the Earth plane.

My Angels explained, *"Little One, your world is about to change. The darker blue of your strand is your service to children up to this moment in Earth's time. Your planet is currently involved in creating, experiencing, and expressing fear in order to learn all that love is not. In order to maintain a world of fear, each life consciousness on Earth is required to learn how to express fear, and then pass all its knowledge and expertise of that fear on to the next generation.*

"Very soon, your planet will undergo the greatest transformation in energy it has ever seen. The pattern of teaching children how to express fear will shift to teaching children how to express love. Even now the children of your planet no longer need to go deeply into fear and are ready for something new. This is the conflict that you feel within yourself, for as the children change you must also change how you serve them."

I asked, "How do I do that, how do I change things?"

They responded, *"Step by step, moment by moment."* I tried to look into the new section of my strand for guidance, but discovered there was no information in it yet. There seemed to be no shortcuts to my destiny on Earth.

Back on Earth, I continued to struggle with my job in light of this new information. A few months later, Michael suggested I leave my position, but I held on. I thought I could get it right, and I was afraid of being unemployed, I had a mortgage now. Then, after two years of service to the agency, I was fired. I had never been fired before and I must admit that while I was relieved, I was also embarrassed.

However, I soon let go of my embarrassment as Michael convinced me that I had actually been fired by my own Spirit. Evidently, trying to be right and doing what I was "supposed to do" had absolutely nothing to do with the wisdom of my Spirit. Once I left the agency, I could feel the shift in my Divine Path. I no longer had to provide services for the children; I simply needed to create a safe place in which each child's Divine Path could unfold.

I found freedom and peace in this realization and was finally able to connect with Michael on a daily basis once again. Immediately, my channeling began to pick up and we developed a rather robust following, as the information I received from Michael became more intricate and accurate for both my clients and me.

Still, finances were tight, and I continued to work part-time, teaching classes and working in retail sales and day care settings. All through college, I had intended to run day care centers and enrichment programs, but I had been drawn into Social Services my first year out of college. This was my chance to return to those dreams.

Being with the kids renewed my own sense of awe and wonder, as the children taught me how to express both love and fear, how to explore the sensuality of this world, and most importantly of all, how to embrace the simple truth that everything that is important in life can be learned through play!

Slowly, in the presence of children, I began to forgive myself for not being perfect. I accepted that it is all right to be afraid and to choose fear. I learned that no human always knows what the loving choice is, and because of that we hurt each other. But most of all, I began to love myself for forgetting Spirit, needing to be right all the time, and for refusing to love myself and my life.

I now understood that each and every experience of my life had been a necessary step in my Divine Path. As I looked back on my life from this new place of forgiveness, I began to see the lessons of my "bad" choices and to share the humor that Michael had so often pointed out to me. Over time, I even realized that I had actually created a safe place within me for my own Divine Path to unfold.

Just as my time in Arizona had allowed me to release old pent up emotions and learn to experience and express my current emotions, this time of my life allowed me to release old thought and behavior patterns, manifest old dreams, and review past decisions.

Growing up in Illinois, I always thought that I would get married and have a family. That had never happened and I had always wondered if I was capable of nurturing a child. My work with the children in Day Care showed me that I did indeed have the capacity to nurture and create a safe haven for children. It also proved, beyond any reasonable doubt, that the road I had taken in my life was the correct one for me.

Step by step, moment by moment, I was beginning to love myself, and that not only brought me closer to Michael, it filled my life with a sense of wholeness and complete happiness. I truly knew who I was and why I was here on this planet.

This process also brought me into alignment with my physical body. Over the years, I had physically healed my anorexia, ulcerated colitis, kidney stones, and walking pneumonia. As I changed my diet and began exercising, I felt much stronger and healthier and was surprised when I started feeling exhausted during the Christmas Holidays of 2005. The problem seemed to worsen and I began to rapidly lose weight.

I could not seem to get an answer from my body as to what was going on, and finally in January of 2006, I asked Michael what was happening. Michael's response was very soft and gentle. *"Your soul is ready to come home. Blue has completed its Divine Path on Earth."*

chapter nine

The Colors Of My Soul

"Your soul is ready to come home." I felt these words more than I heard them, and while I was stunned, strangely enough I was not surprised. I had often said over the course of my life that I would not live past my fifties. I don't know how I knew this—I just did.

So when Michael brought up my physical death, I felt a twinge of excitement. I was making very little money, had no retirement, and was three months away from my fifty-fifth birthday. I knew what the Angelic Realm was and I was ready to go home! Instantly, the last four years made sense to me; I had been finishing up the pieces of my life.

There was a huge sensation of completion, both in the wholeness of my inner being and in the dreams of my outer world. I could think of very little that I wanted to do in this life that I had not already done, and there was a sweet sense of accomplishment and joy. My relationship with Michael was about to take on a whole new significance!

Michael and I began to talk about the transformation and what would happen to my body. I was not afraid of death, but I was terrified of living in pain. Michael told me that I was very anemic and my body was already beginning to break down. He mentioned the possibility that I had aplastic anemia, and then was strangely evasive for several weeks.

I continued to lose weight and just assumed everything was progressing as planned. I didn't have health insurance, but even if the opportunity had been available, I was not interested in medical intervention. My main concern was finding a wonderful home for Buddy, where he would be happy and loved.

Then in the last week of January, Michael spontaneously pulled me into the Angelic Realm during a meditation. For a moment, I actually thought I had died and could stay, but as I started to fly, Michael immediately pulled my consciousness back into my own individualized strand.

I immediately became aware of the huge increase in my strand's vibratory frequency as well as its intensity, depth, and the number of new shades, tints, and hues of blue that had been added since my first visit eleven years ago. Blue was so much larger and fuller than I could have ever imagined, and I loved this soul with every atom of my physical being!

Gently, Michael shifted my focus to a flow of hot pink energy that seemed to be emerging from within Blue. Pink was pretty—I had always loved hot pink—but this energy seemed a little drab and very small next to Blue.

Then Michael said, *"Little One, Blue must return to the Angelic Realm in order to continue its Divine Path. However, your soul has created this pink strand to continue your life on Earth as Viki Hart. As Blue leaves, Pink would like to enter your physical body and utilize all the knowledge and wisdom of Blue as the foundation for its individualized Divine Purpose.*

"Pink's path will be very different from that of Blue, and since each color of your strand has a different vibratory frequency, you will experience a change in personal identity and personality. While these strands differ in many ways, they are extremely compatible and

as a human being, you will experience this as an expansion of Blue's life rather than the end of it. The Divine Purpose of Pink requires that the human be aware of and in agreement with this exchange."

I felt my human mind, body, and emotions immediately scream out, "NO!" as my consciousness returned to Earth. I could not imagine a life without my beautiful blue soul.

Michael gave me a few days before he tried to broach this subject again. We have had many disagreements over the years, and Michael can be very pushy at times, but this was different. This wasn't Michael pushing; this was me refusing to even listen to the possibilities that were being offered.

My mind had learned through years of metaphysical study that when a new soul walks in there is often memory loss, and my human consciousness was adamant that it would not accept another soul taking over and telling it what to do. My physical body was tired and sick and just kept saying, "I can't do this anymore."

However, it was my emotions that I felt the loudest as they screamed over and over, "Blue healed us, and we cannot go on without this light! We cannot survive this planet without Blue!" Never in my life had I felt my mind, body, and emotions so aligned in a decision. I was angry, and I didn't understand what Michael wanted from me.

Physically, mentally, and emotionally exhausted, I finally gave in and agreed to listen to what Michael was trying to say. He explained that Spirit was not proposing the walk-in of another soul. *"Pink is simply another essence of your strand and the difference in vibratory frequency is similar to that of Blue twenty years ago and Blue today. Pink does not want to take over your mind, body, and emotions; it is already a part of them. It simply wants to continue to expand their experience."*

Then Michael said something that shook me to my core. *"Little One, this is not the first time you have shifted souls. Purple left during your kidney surgery when you were thirteen."*

Michael's statement pulled me outside of time. I couldn't breathe, my body was paralyzed, and I was back in the operating room. The doctors were talking about cars with fancy Italian names as I drifted off to sleep and seemed to wake up outside of my body with Archangel Uriel beside me. I liked Uriel—he had brought me to Earth when I was born and always stayed with me when I was sick. He was like a big teddy bear and could always make me laugh at all the things that were going on around me.

We were just hanging out when I saw my purple soul flow out of my body and into the Earth. I knew that my Spirit had left my body and I thought Uriel was taking me home, I was so excited! Only Uriel didn't take me home, and after a lengthy argument, he guided me back into my body.

I awoke from surgery alone and in a great deal of physical pain. I could not remember what Uriel and I had discussed; I only knew that he and the other Angels had left me when my precious soul slipped into the Earth. In my human belief system, that meant my soul had gone to hell not heaven, and I didn't know what I had done that was so wrong that I had to be so severely punished.

Within days of the surgery, I began to lose all conscious memory of this incident, yet it continued to manifest itself in my life from deep within my subconscious. For the next seventeen years, I was lost in the outer world as I desperately tried to be perfect in order to make things right and rescue my soul. No matter what I achieved in school or how many jobs or relationships I had, it was never good enough. I felt no need to nurture myself, and at times I would forget to eat or I would choose to drink Pepsi and smoke cigarettes instead. I did not want to be on this planet, but without a soul there was nowhere else to go.

I thought I would live this hollow existence forever. Then in 1982, my parents took me to Maui. It was a last-minute decision; they were going with a group and found out that if I was willing to sleep on the living room couch of the condo, there was a ticket available. I had always wanted to visit Hawaii and jumped at the chance.

In the predawn hours of our second day, I awoke and immediately knew someone was in the room with me. I turned on the light but no one was there, so I turned it off and tried to go back to sleep. However, that sense of a presence in the room returned, and inside my head I heard my own voice speaking to me. It was an interesting sensation, like thinking someone else's thoughts. The voice told me that I did have a soul and asked me to look for it in the sea.

Later on that rainy afternoon, I was driving along the coast highway with several members of our group when we spotted a humpback whale and her calf in the bay just below us and stopped to watch them. The mother had rolled over on her back and the calf was lying on her stomach. As the mother gently caressed her calf with her pectoral fins, the clouds parted and the sunlight on the water around them took on a brilliant blue hue, almost as if the water had been lit up from below. It was the most beautiful thing I had ever seen and I knew this was the color of my soul!

I returned to Colorado obsessed with finding out more about this blue soul of mine. It took me years to fully connect with and then allow Blue to heal the wounds of my life, and through this process, I learned that no matter what a human believes, feels, or does on this planet; the soul is untouched. Our souls remain pure eternal love unaltered by the fear and darkness of our experiences, silently observing our daily lives until the moment the human is ready to turn and face who we really are.

Still, through all those years of healing, I did not remember Purple, not until the moment Michael revealed to me that I had shifted souls before. Even with this memory in my consciousness, I could not feel Purple, but I did know that my body, mind, and emotions were currently reacting to the loss of Purple rather than the option of accepting Pink. I was completely aligned in fear!

I wanted to leave this planet in the energy of love, so I reluctantly agreed to look at the option of shifting my soul essence. Michael immediately sent me to several holistic practitioners who specialized in nutrition and energy work. All of them received the same information about my health problems, and were asked by Spirit to offer healings that would allow me to stay on the planet if I chose to do so. They also provided relief from the pain, for which my body was very grateful.

Michael then asked me to meet Pink on my turf. In the early 1990s, I had gone to a seminar where our teacher took us through a guided mediation in which we created a place in our imaginations where we could go and meditate. My place started as a small log cabin sitting in a forest on the side of a mountain.

Over the years, the cabin disappeared and my secret place turned into a huge alpine valley with tall rocky peaks surrounding three sides, massive aspen and pine forests, and a waterfall at the far end with a stream running all the way through the valley. I continued to add new wildflowers, grasses, animals, and fluffy white clouds on each of my visits.

I had used this space as a healing center for my mind, body, and emotions, and had even allowed my male, female, and inner child energies to step out of my body and say and do whatever they needed to integrate themselves into the wholeness of my being. At times, I also called my Spirit Guides and Angels into this place to communicate, but in contrast to my visits into the Angelic Realm, this was a physical and human perspective of my life.

I went into meditation and asked Pink to join me. Her presence was huge and she was wearing a headdress that further accentuated her height. Her clothing, headdress, and skin were all a blazing hot pink. She was beautiful, sexy, dynamic, gentle, and very soft with blue eyes and long flowing red hair. Pink was everything that I had always wanted to be and wasn't.

I talked to her openly and honestly about my fears of continuing on without Blue, and she answered all my questions about the changes she would bring to my life. She assured me that together we would continue our path of channeling Michael.

I was intrigued and asked Pink to tell me more about her essence. She told me that she was of Archangel Ariella, a creator of the Earth, who is also known as Mother Earth, the Goddess, Pagea, Pele (who had come to me in Hawaii), and a number of other names among aboriginal tribes.

Pink wished to incarnate on Earth in order to assist mankind in the upcoming shift in its Divine Purpose and to provide the Angelic energy needed to heal the physical planet. As her essence flowed through me, I was completely overwhelmed by the opportunity to live in oneness with Mother Earth. I felt my mind, body, and emotions begin to lean into her energy and release our fears.

Pink was immediately aware of this shift and wrapped me in her energy. From the safety of her love, she explained, *"There are drawbacks to this shift. A new soul essence is easy to bring in, but pulling Blue out will be difficult. You will have health problems during the shift and probably financial difficulties as well. The Spiritual realm will make sure you are taken care of, but your energy will be focused on your physical healing rather than manifesting abundance for several months to come.*

"The transformation of your planet will be uncomfortable as well. As you connect with the very consciousness of Mother Earth and join with her in oneness, you will feel what she feels and experience all that she experiences. Over the next few years, mankind will continue to abuse the planet and do great damage to every inch of her being. It will enrage you and break your heart, but this process is necessary for every life consciousness of Earth to finally see and embrace the truth that humanity and its beautiful planet are one.

"As painful as dealing with humanity will be, the joy will be even greater! As a human, you will become softer, gentler, and more nurturing to yourself and others. You will communicate with Mother Earth as easily as you communicate with other humans. You will travel to the most beautiful and pristine areas of the Earth, providing them with the pure energy of Angelic love that will allow the healing

of all that humanity has inflicted upon it. You will be happy in a way you have not allowed yourself to be as you learn to live in your primal elemental energy without the intrusion of man's fears. You will become all that you were, are, and are meant to be.

"You know in your heart that longevity is built into you and multiple soul essences are a part of your Earth's path in this lifetime, but the choice to stay must be a conscious one made with love."

Pink stepped away and Blue appeared before me and simply said, *"I love you."* Then in the distance, I saw Purple step out of the mist. I had not seen her since the day she slipped into the Earth, and over the last few weeks, I had envisioned her as a fragile child, but she appeared strong and vibrant.

She did not approach me, she merely said, *"I am not who you think I am."* I didn't understand what she meant, and I didn't even try to figure it out. I already knew that I would accept Pink and continue my path on Earth. My reconciliation with Purple would have to wait until another time.

On April 11, 2006, my fifty-fifth birthday, Blue returned to the Angelic Realm. As predicted, the shift was physically difficult. I was weak from the anemia, had no appetite, and just wanted to sleep all the time. A few weeks after the shift, Michael came to me and told me that another soul essence was about to enter. This essence was emerald green and of Archangel Raphael. I was too exhausted to question him and just said okay.

Almost immediately I began to feel better; it seems that Green Guy is an amazing healer! Green Guy is also very fond of Pink Lady and together they created a new sexual energy within me that I thoroughly enjoyed, and by the end of May, I was on the road to regaining my physical strength.

chapter ten

Friends Lost – Friends Found

It's a strange sensation to know that you are literally a different person than you were a few months ago. I wasn't frightened or upset—the process seemed perfectly natural to me—but I was a little surprised. Over the last twenty years, I had changed my belief systems almost as often as I changed my clothes and my hair color. However, I was now beginning to understand that I still believed that a Spirit and a human were separate beings.

Somewhere along the line, I had decided that when a soul entered a physical body it was forced to separate from its source and become human, and only when the human body died could the soul reclaim its true consciousness and universal knowledge. Even with all that Michael had shown me in the Angelic Realm, I still had not grasped the oneness of my spirituality and humanity. However, my shift in soul essences left me no choice but to look at the complexities of this connection more closely.

I discovered almost immediately that the human Viki had become Pink Lady. I looked and sounded the same on the outside, but inside I was totally different. My likes, dislikes, personality, temperament, ideas, opinions, perceptions of the world, and how I felt about almost everything, had changed. I was more outgoing, confident, and comfortable with people and social situations, and the old sensations of walking around with gaping wounds and holes in my energy field quickly melted away. I now knew that I had been waiting for this part of myself all my life.

I did miss Blue and went through a period of grieving, but true to Spirit's promise, I was able to connect with him in meditation. In fact, it was Blue that showed me that our souls and personalities are one. A soul that is outgoing in the Angelic Realm is outgoing on Earth; a more reserved soul creates a more reserved human. Souls that create with a large number of other strands will be comfortable creating with a large number of people, while those souls that prefer to manifest with just a few other strands will choose to do the same on Earth. The soul doesn't create the human personality; our true personality is an expression of the soul.

As I was becoming more and more comfortable with my new personality and life path, my beloved Buddy was suffering. Buddy had always been known as the cruise director of the dog parks and doggie day care centers he attended. He got this title because he was totally obsessed with making sure every dog within a five-mile radius was playing and having a good time.

I had seen Buddy poke, prod, and lick another dog for thirty minutes until it finally gave in and started running and playing. No dog was immune to Buddy's exuberance; he had never failed to ignite doggy joy in every creature he met. Buddy was still playing, but at times, his attention seemed to wane.

As I began to watch and intuitively feel him more closely, I had the sense he was looking and waiting for something. As time went on, the bounce in his step and the amount of time he spent doing what he loved most—running—diminished, and he lost interest in playing with his treats before he ate them. I had him checked out by our vet, and after a clean bill of health, I consulted our Animal Communicator, Jamie McDaniel.

I was crushed by what Buddy told her. Buddy didn't like Pink Lady. He wanted Blue to come back. We tried a variety of clearings, healings, and physical activities to try and help Buddy adjust to the shift, and I even offered to let Buddy go live with another family if he wanted to, but nothing seemed to help.

Finally, I took Buddy into our Sacred Space to meet Pink Lady, and he did politely talk to both Pink Lady and Green Guy, but when he saw Blue on the mountaintop, all he wanted was to climb up to him.

I asked Michael if there was anything else I could do and Michael said, *"No, Little One. All animals have their own Divine Paths. Many animals are Spirits that come to Earth to live totally independent wild lives, while others choose to share their lives with humans as domesticated animals.*

"The majority of animals incarnate from an individualized strand in the Angelic Realm. However, there are also animals, like Buddy, that are created out of a strand that is currently living on Earth. Buddy is Blue, and he came to Earth to teach the human part of you how to love humanity and the world with the innocence of a child, but it is not necessary or appropriate to bring that same energy to Pink. Open you heart to him and let him melt back into Blue."

I cried for two days straight. I was sad, but I was also angry. Michael and Pink Lady had not mentioned the possibility of losing Buddy in this shift. Granted, I had not asked, but this relationship was the most important one I had on Earth. Buddy was my child, companion, protector, confidant, and playmate. Still, I knew Michael was right, so Jamie and I both talked to Buddy and I gave him permission to leave.

Then I panicked! Buddy was young and healthy, and I didn't know how he was going to make his transition. Every time we walked out the door, I was afraid he would get hit by a car, find something poisonous to eat, or we would get mugged and Buddy would be killed protecting me. I was totally irrational for five excruciating days until I awoke one morning with Buddy standing over me in the bed.

In the first few seconds of coming out of a deep sleep, I actually thought that Buddy was someone else. I didn't think he was another dog; I actually felt another presence standing over me. He then bounded out of bed and began barking to go outside. His depression of the last month definitely seemed to have lifted.

Over the next week, Buddy began to refuse to eat his normal food and became rather pushy about wanting to eat whatever I had on my plate. I tried several new dog foods and finally found one to his liking. His energy was extremely high, even for an Aussie, and he seemed different—more confident, mature, and focused.

Buddy had always had some very obsessive behaviors, and everyone that met him thought he was ADD, but that behavior seemed to disappear overnight. While I found that restful, it was also a little unsettling, and I continued to be unnerved about the way he felt to me. Buddy was very skinny with long legs, and while his weight had not changed, he seemed to be thicker and more solid.

I kept asking Michael if Buddy was okay and was continually assured everything was fine. Then one afternoon, I went into my sacred place and saw Buddy sitting on top of the mountain with Blue and felt a rush of warmth in my heart; they were so happy together!

I wanted to give them some time alone and as I turned away, I saw a huge brown and white horse coming towards me. As it came nearer, I was stunned to realize that it was not a horse, it was Buddy! He came right up to me and asked me to get on and go for a ride, as I demanded to know who he was. He responded that he was "Big Bud" and he had slipped into "Little Bud's" body when he left.

I climbed on, and during our ride Buddy explained that he was a part of Green Guy and had the ability to diagnosis illnesses and other problems in the human body and determine possible cures. He immediately offered to help me expand my channeled readings and healings. This Bud was not my child, this Bud was my partner!

Archangel Michael confirmed this information, and Buddy even did a very accurate reading for the animal communicator during one of their sessions. I must admit that the idea of a soul shift in a dog coupled with the fact that my dog could now do readings and get information that I couldn't, drove me a little crazy for a few days.

I kept asking Michael where Buddy got his information and Michael kept answering, *"Where do you get yours?"* Finally, I realized that my belief that people and animals are spiritually different was incorrect, and I just let it go. Once I accepted this, Buddy and I settled into a wonderful partnership, and he has been assisting me with my readings ever since.

My relationships with the rest of the world turned out to be a little more difficult to deal with. Blue was a very soft essence that enjoyed expressing a lot of male energy on the planet. I did not particularly like being a girl; I had always felt that men had more power in the world and it was not safe to be a woman.

By the time I reached my thirties, I had hidden my goddess energy so deep within me that even I had difficulty finding it. In addition, my Divine Path with Blue had been dominated by the experience of the perpetrator/victim energy pattern. I had learned as a young child that being the victim of a kidney disease and my older brother's teasing got me attention and the things I wanted. Later in life, I discovered that I could also get what I wanted by manipulating and controlling others as a perpetrator.

While I now understood that the victim and perpetrator are trapped in the same energy, I spent most of my life trying to feel better about myself by playing whichever role seemed to be the most effective in the moment. It never really occurred to me that there was another way to live until Pink Lady came along.

Pink Lady's Divine Path is dominated by the expression of female energy, and does not include victim/perpetrator patterns. As Pink Lady, I knew who I was, what I was thinking, and what it felt like to be me. However, I also retained the memories of what I had done, thought, and felt prior to my shift, but no matter how hard I tried, I just could not align my past with my present life. It was like remembering my childhood as an adult, the memories are wonderful, but I am no longer that child.

Without warning, there were behaviors, feelings, thoughts, ideas, and judgments that I could no longer tolerate in my relationships, and one by one, my friendships and professional relationships seemed to fall away.

Luckily, a few relationships did survive and began to deepen. Three in particular continued to bring joy and comfort into my life. All of these wonderful women are aware of what happened to me and have been able to deal with the difficulties my spiritual path has created in my daily life.

Marsha Sterling, who I have worked with since the late 1980s, is not only the most positive person I have ever known, she is also a good friend of Michael's and a gifted healer. Marsha walked through my soul shifts with me without blinking an eye. The journey of my life could not have succeeded without her wonderful healings and guidance.

Suzanne Pittman also continued to provide a sane voice at the other end of a phone line, and her long distance Reiki healings surrounded my craziest moments with a sense of calm acceptance.

I had known Nancy Hart for only about a year when Pink Lady entered, and I immediately recognized her as a soul mate. Blue had liked Nancy, but Pink Lady knew Nancy! Nancy is not only positive, she is fun, hot, and a girly girl, all of the things that Pink Lady admires in the human race.

Pink Lady really opened my heart to these three women and I am so lucky to have them in my life. They kept me on track as my old life was melting away and still support me in all that I do, regardless of the color of my hair!

Naturally, Michael was not fazed by my change in personality and I found this very comforting in the chaos surrounding my life. It was as if nothing between us had changed at all.

That is, until he came to me in the first week of June and said, *"You asked if we could create a pocket of Angelic energy so that people could sit in it and feel it on their skin; we can do that now."* And with those words, my journey on Earth took off in a whole new direction!

chapter eleven

Agnes Vaille Falls

Life is sweeter when you know you have chosen your own path; even the bad times are easier. There is always a sense of hopelessness about believing that someone else has decided your fate. When things are bad, there is nothing you can do to change them, and when things are good, you never know when someone will decide to take it all away.

However, when you are making your own decisions and everything starts going wrong, you have the power to change things, and when they go right you have to ability to continue on your course. Now some people may say that it is both stressful and tiring to have to make all the decisions in their daily lives, but I think that statement is more about having to make choices for others and trying to make everyone else happy with your choices.

Pink Lady brought a new power, confidence, and trust into the choices I was making in my life. Perhaps it was just the release of the victim/perpetrator energy, or perhaps it was something I had yet to discover about my new life, but I was no longer afraid of living on Earth. I was blessed with being able to start life anew with the grace and wisdom of my past intact. It was rather delightful to be able to avoid pain by knowing what not to do.

As my physical health continued to improve, I began the day-to-day chores of putting my life in order. I had been able to work only sporadically during the last few months, so finances were first on the agenda. As I started looking for a job, I discovered that the work I had done in the past no longer seemed to fit my interests and who I was, but I also needed my past resume to find a new position. Michael assured me that this conflict didn't matter at this point in my life and suggested I just take the job that paid the most, so I started sending out resumes.

Next on the agenda was finding out more about Michael's statement that we could now create a pocket of Angelic energy on the Earth plane. He explained, *"Little One, your planet is about to undergo a great shift in its Divine Purpose, which will allow the Earth and Angelic Realm to interact in new ways. When you asked if you could create a pocket of Angelic energy on the Earth, your soul agreed to try, but it will take a minimum of six soul essences to do so.*

"Pink and Green are fully integrated into your physical being, Purple is connected to you from the etheric web that lies within the center of the Earth, and Blue remains aligned with you in the Angelic Realm. In addition, two other soul essences, Orange and Yellow, have been created and are now flowing through you in the Angelic Realm and may choose, in the future, to integrate into your physical body." Great, more company on the way!

"Your soul is proposing that we create a bubble on Earth in which Angelic energy can flow freely. The Angelic energy will not replace the physical energy; it will merely share the same space with it. It is similar to how the Angelic Realm originally created the physical universe within its oneness, and just as the physical universe needs a boundary to contain it, so does this area.

"The boundary that is created on Earth must include energy from both the physical and Angelic Realms and be capable of increasing

its vibratory frequency and expanding in size through Earth's linear time. Once the pocket is created, it will exist as long as the physical Earth exists.

"Your physical body now has the capability of creating a matrix in which to place the energy. By pulling the energy of your six soul essences through your DNA, your Spirit can weave its brightly colored energy into a physical form. Visualize this matrix as a cylinder sitting on the Earth with one end attached to the Angelic Realm by Blue and the other end attached to the etheric web in the center of the Earth by Purple. Once the cylinder is attached at both ends, we will open a doorway in its center and allow Angelic energy to flow into the Earth plane. As the vibratory frequency of the Earth continues to increase over time, the cylinder will naturally expand outward into your world.

"Once the cylinder is created within your body, we will tell you where to place it. You will need to do a ritual to pull the matrix out of your body and then offer it to your planet as an eternal gift of love. Angelic energy is non-intrusive, so anyone entering the space will have to ask for the energy to experience it. This request may come from the human or the Spirit within, so it is not necessary that individual humans are aware of the matrix to enjoy it.

"Animals, plants, rocks, water, and the entire natural world will also have access to the energy of the matrix. You asked to create a place in which humans could feel the Angelic energy outside of their bodies and on their skin. Are you ready to create an Angelic Doorway?"

This was not at all what I had expected when I asked the question, but I was excited and asked Michael what I needed to do. Over the next few days, Michael explained to me that my Spirit would create the matrix, but I needed to immediately start preparing myself physically, mentally, and emotionally to release the cylinder through a sacred ritual.

The first step required that I lose ten pounds, complete one hour of aerobic exercise and fifteen minutes of strength training each day, and eat a piece of dark chocolate every night before bedtime. Luckily, I had lost a lot of weight prior to and during the shift of my soul essences, so this weight loss simply continued without interruption. I still felt weak, but surprisingly, the exercise was very easy for me to handle. I do not like to exercise or sweat, but I will do anything for chocolate, and my body responded to both with an attitude of joy. I found that I could talk to my body and channel Michael during my exercise sessions and that was fun! Within a week, I actually began to crave this special time.

The second step was to prepare my mind. Michael asked me to set intentions for the ritual, and I immediately knew that I wanted to offer my love to humanity. I had spent most of my life harshly judging humanity for creating, embracing, and using fear to destroy each other and the natural world that I loved. Over the last few years, Michael had shown me that my species isn't naturally destructive; fear is destructive. I now understood that Spirit required all life on Earth to learn about fear in order to make the choice to love, and I wanted to both celebrate and honor the courageous path all humans have undertaken. My intentions were simple and easy, and I finished them within a few days.

Soon things got interesting. To create these intentions, all of my thoughts, beliefs, and ideas had to be in alignment with what I was asking. I was stunned to find out how many misconceptions I had, as belief after belief entered my mind and began to appear in the words and actions of those around me. After a few crazy and frustrating days of trying to process all these beliefs, Michael suggested that I just surrender them to Spirit.

He explained, *"When a human mind processes a belief by examining what it is, where it comes from, and how you feel about it, the belief actually manifests in the outer world as an opportunity for you to make the choice to maintain or release it. This form of manifestation takes a great deal of time and energy. However, you*

*have the ability to simply acknowledge the belief and ask Spirit to
take it from you, which is much easier and faster."*

I began to try this and it was amazing. It seemed to take no
energy at all and my belief systems shifted within minutes rather
than days.

The final step of aligning my emotions took a similar path. As I
become overwhelmed with past emotions, I began to acknowledge
that I felt fear, anger, sadness, etc. and then requested, "If this
emotion is not of this moment, please take it from me now." At first,
it would take two to three hours to release an emotion, but after a few
weeks, I was feeling relief within thirty minutes. This simple form
of surrendering to Spirit has made my life much easier and happier
through the years, and anyone can do it.

I completed my preparations, intentions, and ritual the last week
in June, and Michael informed me the doorway would be opened at
Mt. Princeton. Michael then explained, *"The matrix will be placed
in a box canyon, which will help to contain it and prevent it from
expanding too rapidly. The actual doorway will be opened behind
a waterfall so that as the Angelic energy enters the physical realm,
it can be dampened by the water. The water will also serve to carry
the Angelic energy out of the canyon and eventually into the Gulf of
Mexico."*

Mt. Princeton is well known for its Hot Springs, and I had been
to the area many times. I quickly got on the computer and googled
Colorado waterfalls and found Agnes Vaille Falls, an eighty-foot
waterfall dropping into a box canyon five miles west of the hot
springs that I had used during my shamanic training in the early
1990s. Michael confirmed the location and asked that I open the
doorway at dawn of the next full moon. I made the arrangements and
on July 10th drove to Mt. Princeton resort to spend the night.

I was excited and went to bed early since I had to be up by five the
next morning. I was fast asleep when Michael entered my dreams and

told me to wake up. I sat up in bed and looked at the clock and saw it was shortly after midnight when Michael said, *"It has begun."*

He then asked me to take the covers off and turn towards the door, and as I did I was completely bathed in the moonlight that was entering through the dormer windows above the door. I could actually feel the cool softness of the moonlight on my skin and fell asleep wrapped in Michael's energy.

The alarm clock was jarring, and I literally jumped out of bed and almost fell over. I was not dizzy, but I had absolutely no sense of balance and had to hold onto the bed and dresser to get to the bathroom. I heard Michael telling me to slow down; the Angels had pulled most of my energy out of my body. He also seemed to be saying that as I got closer to the falls, I would walk into my energy and feel better, but I was too busy trying to stand up and get dressed to really listen.

I was somehow able to maneuver my body and backpack into the car, and by the time I had driven the five miles to the trailhead, I did feel better. I practically ran up the half-mile trail with its 450-foot ascent, with Michael again telling me to slow down, and arrived at the top of the canyon a few minutes before the first rays of sunshine appeared on the rocks above.

It was July, but I was above nine thousand feet in elevation, and the temperature was still in the forties. The area around the falls was filled with rocks that had fallen from the steep canyon walls, and it took me a few minutes to find a small level area directly in front of the falls where I could perform my ritual.

The first part of the ritual required me to ask permission of the Angelic Realm and Mother Earth to open the doorway. I raised my hands towards the top of the waterfall and simply asked, "Do I have permission to open a doorway to the Angelic Realm?" I expected a simple yes, but the yes was accompanied by a thank you that seemed to echo through my body hundreds, thousands, and perhaps even millions of times.

I was in my body on Earth, yet I felt as if I was melting into the oneness of pure love. As the Angelic waves of gratitude overwhelmed my physical body, my knees buckled, and I found myself on the ground sobbing uncontrollably and gasping for air. My mind could not comprehend that the Angelic Realm had just thanked me, a simple human being, for what we were about to do, and my emotions were struggling to embrace the full force of my spiritual essence as it flowed through me for the first time on Earth.

I don't know how long I laid on the ground crying, but eventually my body, mind, and emotions seemed to embrace what was happening, and I was able to sit up and place my palms on the ground and ask Mother Earth's permission. I again heard yes, but this time I felt a soft tremble of energy move through me like a desperate plea. Mother Earth not only wanted this energy, she needed it, and that gave me the strength to stand up and continue the ritual.

I opened my chakras and pulled the matrix out of my body with the intention, "I surrender to the power and presence of God within me," and then stated my personal intentions. As I finished, Michael asked me to add an intention. I had already asked to walk the Earth with Angels, but Michael wanted me to ask to walk the Earth as an Angel. Without thinking, I made this request.

Michael then asked me to sit down and close my eyes. I was immediately in the Angelic Realm with Michael, Uriel, Gabrielle, Raphael, and Ariella at my side. However, I could not seem to move, and after what seemed like a few minutes, Michael asked me to open my eyes. I thought this was really funny because I didn't have eyes in the Angelic Realm, but my physical body responded.

I immediately saw rain falling about fifty yards in front of me and wondered why I wasn't getting wet. I started laughing as I realized the rain was really a flow of hot pink drops of Angelic energy with blue, purple, orange, green, and yellow drops flowing in and out of the pink. I watched as the rain slowly curved itself around me into the shape of a cylinder that was about one hundred yards in diameter.

The birds in the area of the waterfall began chirping very loudly and flying up to the edge of the cylinder, but they would not fly through it. Several chipmunks also came out to see what was happening and walked up to the edge, stopped, and then continued on their way, seemingly unaffected as they walked right through the energy wall.

As I felt the familiar warmth of Angelic energy begin to surround me, I could not keep my eyes open. I was home in the Angelic Realm and I simply wanted to bask in the experience. There was no sense of time, and I quickly lost all awareness of my body.

Michael then called to me and asked me to open my eyes again. I could no longer see the cylinder, and Michael told me to get up and return to the resort. I could hear him, but I didn't seem to have the capacity to follow his instructions and just sat there. He kept telling me over and over that my energy had expanded too far out of my body and that my body was cold and needed to be warmed up; but I was happy and didn't care. He then suggested I eat the chocolate bar that I had brought with me and I readily complied.

Chocolate is a wonderful thing, and after finishing off the whole bar, I was able to get up, walk down the trail, and get in the car. Over two hours had passed and I suddenly realized I was shivering from the cold. I returned to the resort, had breakfast, and then got into the hot springs.

Four hours later, my energy had completely pulled back into the vicinity of my body, and while I was extremely happy, my body was feeling the heat of my nasty sunburn. I learned that day that it is very important to pay attention to where you leave your body while visiting the Angelic Realm!

chapter twelve

The Angelic Movement

Gift giving is an art form. My mother was very good at it, but my friend Nancy Hart is a true artist of giving. I'm supposed to be the psychic in our friendship, but it is Nancy who always gives me the perfect gift, the one I have been secretly asking for. I have observed her closely on our shopping trips, trying to learn the secret of her ability to pick out just the right gift for each person in her life.

So far, I have been able to identify only three of her magical abilities. The first is that she listens to what people are saying, and the second is that she observes them to see what they pause to look at, touch, eat, listen to, and even smell. The third seems to be a combination of perfect timing and the ability to visualize how the gift and the person will melt into each other. For example, will this particular gift bring joy, comfort, playfulness, a sense of fulfillment, or even inspire sensual or sexual feelings? I sometimes want to ask her if the gift is actually talking to her, but that just seems too weird even for our relationship.

I, on the other hand, have a tendency to give gifts to others that I want. It's not that I don't want to give the perfect gift or take hours agonizing over what to choose, I just can't seem to visualize the person with the gift. So I shouldn't have been surprised when the gift that I asked to give humanity and the gift that the Angelic and physical realms delivered were somewhat different! Spirit had just given me the gift that I truly wanted!

Channeling Michael changed my life not just because of the information that I received but also because of the love in which it was given. There is nothing that Michael has said to me that has not been said on Earth before, but when coupled with the love of Michael and the Angelic Realm, I could feel myself as a Spirit. I was able to enter my infinite eternal self, and that is what I thought I wanted to offer other humans.

What I did not realize was that in entering this state, I was actually leaving my humanity and the physical world behind. My human body can't enter the Angelic Realm and melt into the pure love of oneness, but the Angelic Doorway had just allowed that pure energy of love to enter the physical Earth. The gift I had been given was not to offer humans a spiritual experience, or even to allow Spirit a human experience; it was to create the possibility of melting these two experiences together on the Earth plane.

I wanted to take credit for this amazing gift and embrace myself as a truly powerful spiritual being, but I knew that I didn't have a clue what was going on. I didn't even know what questions to ask Michael to try and make sense of what had happened on the mountain that morning. So I ate dinner, slept, and the next day, I drove home.

It only took about twenty minutes of driving to realize that something had also changed between Michael and me. For several years, I had been able to feel Michael's presence beside me whenever I asked. His energy was soft, warm, and as light as a soft breeze caressing my cheek, and our communication required only that I ask a question and pause to listen for the answer. I had even learned to visualized an on/off switch in my head that sped up our initial connection, but our conversations still felt choppy at times and took a great deal of conscious effort on my part. That was about to change!

I started thinking about Buddy and wondering if the storms that had been predicted for Colorado Springs had actually hit, and if so, had he had been too scared to eat or sleep. Michael immediately said, *"No the storms went north and Buddy is having a great time playing."*

I was so startled that I jumped and actually turned to the passenger's seat and said out loud, "Michael, you scared me." I could feel—but not see—a very physical presence next to me, while at the same time feeling Michael's energy inside of me. It felt as if Michael had gone from monotone to stereo.

I laughed at myself for talking out loud to Michael, and he responded, *"I like hearing your voice."* Now I was a little freaked out! Reaching out for an Angel is one thing, having one physically in your face is another.

I asked Michael what was going on and he explained, *"You created the matrix within your body and then expanded it out into your physical world. That is the way your physical world is created, from the inside out. However, the original matrix or creation always remains within you as a part of your physical being. When we opened the permanent doorway in the matrix of the natural world, we also opened a permanent doorway within your individual body as well.*

"This makes it appear to your physical senses that we are speaking to you from inside and outside of your body at the same time. While this has never been done on the Earth in this way before, the Angelic Realm is hoping it will create a new form of communication between humans and Angels, because if we can achieve this with you, we can achieve it with all humans. How does it feel to you?"

"I feel like I'm talking to another physical being."

"A very warm intelligent being, I hope."

"Michael, are you and the Angelic Realm using me as a guinea pig?"

Michael and I have been dialoguing ever since that day, and there are even times when we get really excited and talk over each other. One of the great things about this new way of communicating is that Michael can initiate a conversation. Michael often directs my attention to a flower or an animal that I would have otherwise missed on my walks, and he is very good about giving me driving directions before I realize I'm lost. Time and time again, Michael will tell me to turn on the TV or radio and listen to a certain song or show, and he always seems to have my shopping list memorized in case I forget it.

It's heartwarming to be comforted without having to ask for it, exciting to have a stimulating conversation during a boring business meeting, and very efficient to be able to talk to Michael with my mouth full!

The gift of opening the Angelic Doorway at Agnes Vaille Falls truly allowed me to walk the Earth with Angels, but perhaps more importantly, it taught me how to love myself as a human. For as long as I can remember, I have tried to escape from the pain and suffering of Earth by stripping away every layer of fear from my mind, body, and emotions in an attempt to become worthy of entering the Angelic Realm and reclaiming the pure love of my Angelhood.

I spent years searching, studying, and practicing numerous ways of moving my consciousness out of my body in order to touch and channel the energy and knowledge of Spirit, until that day in July 2006, when I reversed the process and asked to bring the love of the Angelic Realm here to Earth, and everything inside of me changed in an instant.

Over the next few months, I questioned Michael about what had happened to me as a result of opening the doorway. He explained, *"Little One, you have entered the Angelic Movement, and the rest of your planet is about to join you. The Angelic Movement is also known as the Paradigm Shift, the Prophesy, the End Days, as well as many other catchy phrases. We call it the Angelic Movement because it is about moving the energy of the Angelic Realm directly into the Earth plane.*

"The current Divine Purpose of Earth is to learn about fear, but fear cannot exist in the vibratory frequency of love, so spiritual energy had to be slowed down and compressed to create the density of fear in your physical world. Since the beginning of Earth, all its life consciousness has used this slower energy to create, explore, and play with fear, and we would like to congratulate you. You have mastered the fine art of fear.

"Within a few Earth months, the last consciousness in the One Soul of Earth will finish its lessons with fear and at that moment, the Divine Purpose of Earth will change. The Earth will shift its focus from fear to love, and you will begin to take your first steps towards learning how to express Divine Love on Earth.

"This process will occur through an increase in the vibratory frequency of every life consciousness on Earth to a level that is compatible with the vibratory frequency of the Angelic Realm. Many humans refer to this process as Enlightenment and experience the process as stripping away or releasing experiences, thoughts, feelings, and behaviors of fear. However, the Angelic Movement is actually created by expressing love. Every time an individual life consciousness expresses love, their vibratory frequency increases.

"Releasing fear does not raise one's vibratory frequency, but it does help to create space in which love can then flow. It may be helpful for you to know that you can feel intense fear and still raise your energy by choosing to express love in each moment. On the other hand, if you continue to focus all your attention on getting rid of your fears, you will remain at that lower vibratory frequency."

"So what does this doorway inside and outside of me have to do with this process?"

"This shift in focus has never taken place on the Earth before. It has been unsuccessfully attempted many times in the past, and each time, the consciousness of the One Soul of Earth learned more and

more about how to successfully shift its energy. The last attempt was in the time of Atlantis, when Mother Earth was physically torn apart by a split in human consciousness.

"Think of the energy of the Earth as a wine glass and the energy of the Angelic Realm as a symphony. Most of the notes played in the symphony will not affect the glass; however, there are certain tones (vibratory frequencies) that can actually shatter the glass. In Atlantis, humanity was in discord with itself and Mother Earth when it attempted to pull the Angelic energy into the physical plane prematurely. This resulted in the shattering of both the tectonic plates of Earth and the connection of the mind, body, and emotions of humans. The memory of this experience lies within the DNA of many people on Earth, resulting in the fear and beliefs known as the End Days prophesy.

"The doorway is designed to both align the energies of the two realms and act as a safety valve. The vibratory frequency of the natural world of Earth is much higher than that of humanity. In other words, humans hold more fear in their physical bodies than do the animals, plants, rocks, water, electricity, etc. on your planet.

"The doorway allows Angelic energy to enter the natural world and your human body simultaneously, by adjusting the vibratory frequencies and energy flows to maintain your physical compatibility with the planet."

"So you are using me as a guinea pig.*"*

"No Little One, you are a highly trained volunteer. Angelic energy is non-intrusive; you must invite the energy in and then allow the doorway to automatically adjust the flow of energy into the physical plane from the Angelic side. The doorway also gives you the ability to enter the Angelic Realm whenever you choose and to open a temporary doorway anywhere on Earth."

I had to admit that that sounded like fun. It seemed that my request to let my clients feel Michael's energy on their skin may have been granted after all!

chapter thirteen

Angel Speak

I stopped struggling the day the Angelic Doorway opened. I did retain the right to worry—after all, a girl can't give up everything on a moment's notice—but I did stop fighting all the details of Earth that my humanity perceived as abusive, unfair, or unjust. I was not sure if this was the final release of my old victim/perpetrator patterns, or if I had just become so enthralled with the knowledge that I could now bring the essence of love into my physical world that nothing else seemed to matter.

Whatever it was, it altered my perceptions of the world around me. The day I returned from the falls, I received a call to interview for a full-time position working with infants. I was concerned that this job was not compatible with my current life and belief systems, and Michael agreed.

However, he assured me that the purpose of this job was to maintain me financially and allow me to pay off all my debts in the next few months and explained, *"You and the planet are not yet ready to unfold your new Divine Purpose. Relax, have fun, and let all that is to be simply come to you."*

This job did test my patience. Within a few weeks, the other teacher in my room quit and was not replaced for five months. In the past, I would have tried to meet the needs of all the families in the program by working twice as many hours, but I had given up struggling with the outer world and simply did what I could do and left the other half undone. Strangely enough, no one died and I learned, once and for all, that I am not responsible for meeting the needs of the entire world.

This new approach to work left me with more than enough time to focus on my life with Michael and the Angelic Realm. However, I soon discovered that trying to join two realms in one's daily life is a little like trying to create a marriage when the bride and groom are from two different cultures and speak two different languages.

Even in deep meditation, there had been many times when I was unsure of what Michael was really saying to me, and I soon found that I was totally inept at sustaining ongoing communications in our daily relationship. Michael understood English (and every other language on Earth) very well, but much of what we shared could not be conveyed within the limitations of human language.

I needed to learn how to communicate in the language of Angels (which I aptly named Angel Speak), and Michael agreed to teach me the basics of his beautiful and sensitive language of spiritual love.

Angel Speak is the flow of energy between the individualized strands of the Angelic Realm. All life consciousnesses of Earth—whether human, plant, animal, mineral, elemental, etc—are born with this language; however, few humans seem to remember it past the age of two or three. My experiences with human babies led me to believe that we forget or shut off this flow of energy as we learn human language.

I must also admit that many of my attempts to connect with babies failed, causing me to wonder if there is something unique about each human's soul language. I asked Michael why it is so much more difficult for humans to connect with Spirit than it is for other forms of life consciousness on the planet.

"Little One, humanity chose to experience fear on a much deeper level than the rest of your planet. It was a loving and courageous choice that plunged your species into a great deal of pain and suffering.

"In order to separate from the natural world, humanity created a collective consciousness at a lower vibratory frequency than the rest of the planet, and then used this lower energy to create its experiences. The human mind literally created a new set of languages and symbols that would allow it to easily communicate with each other, while further separating it from the rest of the life consciousness of your planet.

"This process created an unexpected side effect for humanity. Individuals were now forced to pull their higher spiritual energy through the lower vibratory frequencies of the human mind, which reduced its speed. Slowing the energy down changes how it looks, feels, and sounds, or in other words how it is experienced.

"Over time, the human mind began to define these lower energies as Divine Love and assimilate all spiritual knowledge into its limitations. Humanity began to see God in human form rather than humans as individualized expressions of God!

"If you want to speak Angel on Earth, you must reverse the process. You must allow the spiritual energy to flow through your physical being at its higher vibratory frequency and allow it to create new perceptions, concepts, experiences, and words of Divine Love. This new language will be based on your individual life experiences on Earth and with other realms in this particular lifetime, and therefore, will be unique to Viki Hart.

"Since your path includes translating the universal knowledge of the Angelic Realm into human language, your language will differ from those who paint their visions; sing their HeartSongs; heal the physical mind, body, and emotions; create loving homes and communities; and all other expression of love. Every human on

Earth will soon create a unique version of Angel Speak that best suits their new Divine Path."

Michael and I began creating the language of our relationship with one simple step. *"Little One, every human on Earth can connect with the Angels simply by meditating for five minutes in the morning and five minutes at night. Angels have always been able to enter your dream states and give you information and love. However, your conscious states have been focused on fear and its experiences, and through time your brains have learned to shut us out during your waking hours.*

"You can change that merely by asking. When you meditate upon waking and ask us to communicate with you during the day, our information continues to flow into your waking consciousness. And when you offer gratitude and thanksgiving just before you sleep, the cycle can continue twenty-four hours a day."

I tried this method of meditation and found it to be easy, efficient, and much more effective than the hours of mediation that I had been doing for the past ten years. Now I simply start my day by asking for what I want, listening to Michael's suggestions, and feeling loved, before I even get out of bed. It makes my day much more joyful, and by the time I crawl into bed, I am more than ready to say thank you and ask for any information, healing, or just the rest that I need during the night. There are still many times when I do deep meditation, but these simple five-minute prayers have enriched my life beyond belief.

I have also found a few other ways to easily connect with Angels that I would like to share with anyone who might be interested. Begging, yelling, and groveling are extremely effective in getting their attention! I can't tell you the number of times that I have quietly prayed for an answer or solution to a problem, only to receive silence for days on end. Then in desperation, I began to cry, scream, stomp my feet, and at times even throw things and miraculously received a response.

I don't know if extreme emotions allow Angels to respond more quickly or if they just need to be convinced that we are really serious about needing their help, but if you want help it's okay to demand it. Another key to making connections with Angels is to ask questions. The energy of the Angelic Realm feels very much like the curiosity of humans, and any question that you ask immediately draws attention to you and begins a conversation.

Learning the language of Angels allowed me to continuously feel their Divine Love, and I soon recognized that the greatest gift of this energy is its ability to flow through my body, mind, and emotions, imbuing every action, thought, and feeling that I experienced with love. It allowed me to perceive the world around me as the Angels do, from a place of pure love.

Once I began to see, feel, hear, taste, and even smell the Divine Love in every physical form that surrounded me, my human perceptions and experiences took on new meaning and wisdom. I learned to love what I once feared, and intuitively knew that I could create oneness on Earth by sharing my loving experiences with both Angels and other humans.

As I continued to expand my version of Angel Speak during the last half of 2006, I became aware of the shifting of our planet's energy. It was exciting and terrifying all at the same time. I knew we were ready, and still I was afraid we might not make it.

I went to work during the week and observed the unkind words and behaviors that accompanied fear. On weekends, I went to Agnes Vaille Falls, sat in the matrix, and watched how people responded to the new energy flowing gently into our physical home. It was amusing to watch as some people came to the edge of the cylinder and stopped, unable to take their first step into the new possibilities of life. It was reassuring to see others plunge into the core of the energy and quietly draw in its softness through play and meditation.

Children and animals often ran wildly around the area, while a few people seemed to feel invincible within the energy as they tried to climb the steep walls of the canyon, which were clearly marked, "DANGER FALLING ROCKS." Unfortunately, it appears that proximity to the Angelic Realm does not inhibit stupidity!

Michael also taught me how to temporarily open the matrix in my home. However, whenever I did this, Buddy came charging into the room barking and demanding to go outside. After a few sessions with the Animal Communicator, we figured out that the matrix emitted a very low frequency sound and caused a barometric pressure change in the house that hurt Buddy's ears, so I was only able to open the matrix and enter the Angelic Realm a few times, when Buddy was at Doggy Day Care or the groomers.

Then in mid-October, I was relaxing at the falls when Michael told me this would be my last trip of the year. He informed me that the weather was going to get very harsh soon and it would not be safe to hike up the trail until March. He was right; we had one snowstorm after another that winter, and travel was impossible.

Even though our channeled readings steadily increased through the fall, I found myself longing for something more over the holidays. I missed the matrix and the Angelic Realm and was becoming more and more disconnected at my job. I longed for something new and exciting, yet I felt that I had no greater gift to give to my planet than the Angelic Doorway. Michael softly and gently encouraged me to dive into the depths of my longing and I reluctantly did.

Then in the second week of January 2007, he quietly said, *"Little One, the paradigm shift has occurred. The Divine Purpose of Earth has changed, and it is time for you to begin learning how to express all the infinite love that you are in the physical plane!"*

chapter fourteen

An Angelic Perspective

"The Paradigm Shift has occurred." Those words immediately transported me back to an operating room in 1964. My purple soul had just flowed into the Earth, and I was arguing with Archangel Uriel. I must admit that I was impressed with my ability to take on an Archangel with such ferocity. My energy field was tiny compared to his, but that did not stop me; I was not about to allow Purple to move on without me.

Uriel let me express absolutely everything my human consciousness could think of and then gently said, *"Little One, Purple must leave your physical body for you to complete your Divine Plan in this lifetime. Have you totally forgotten why you came to Earth at this point in its history?"* Evidently, I had.

"You have come to assist the Earth in shifting its Divine Purpose. You have been on Earth for every attempted shift in its history." I was slowly beginning to remember. *"Your second Divine Path in this lifetime is to join your Angelic and human energies into oneness, to merge the expression of Divine and human love, and to walk the Earth as an Angel/human for the first time.*

"However, in order to accomplish this, you must first finish your

work with fear. This requires you to believe that you have been totally separated from God and the Angelic Realm. You must walk the Earth believing that you are totally alone, perhaps even abandoned. We know this will be painful, and your human heart will be broken into a thousand pieces over and over again. We want you to know that while you will forget us, we will never forget you. When the consciousness of the planet reaches the vibratory frequency required for the Angelic Movement to take hold, we will awaken you and bring you back into oneness with the Angelic Realm."

Looking down at my body on the operating table, I remembered everything, and with great excitement chose to stay on Earth as Blue and dive as deeply into the experience of fear and aloneness as my human mind would allow. Looking back, I have to wonder if there wasn't an easier way of doing things, but my soul is what my soul is, and after all, I did survive!

The sudden realization that I had chosen to stay on Earth without Purple lifted a tremendous weight from my being. My fear of being in trouble every time Uriel appeared melted away, and the childhood love that I had felt for this teddy bear of an Angel flooded back into my physical being. I could feel Uriel wrap his energy around me and I leaned into him for the first time in over forty years.

This Angel's love is huge and transformative, and within moments, years of fear and aloneness simply dissolved away. I spent the next few days reconnecting with Uriel both on Earth and in the Angelic Realm and allowing all those pieces of my heart to melt back into wholeness.

Michael delighted in our reconnection. After all Michael perceives all Angels as one so as I connected with Uriel, I connected more deeply with Michael. As Michael and I began to talk about the paradigm shift, I soon realized that the depression of the last few months was more about the past than the present.

I began to remember my first incarnation on Earth as Xyla, a bird woman from another planet. We actually thought we would come to Earth to experience a little fear and complete the shift in one generation, but we created a war instead. Then there was Caras, a sixteen-year-old high priestess in Atlantis whose purpose had been similar to that of this lifetime. I remembered standing on a mountaintop, believing that we had succeeded, when the first earthquake hit and I lost everyone I loved and was responsible for protecting.

The pain of those lives and many more flowed through my heart, and Michael reached out and took them from me, and as he did, my depression lifted. I had waited all my life for this moment in history and seemed to be holding my breath, waiting for fear to drag me back into its grip once again. I needed to know why we had succeeded this time when we had failed so many times before.

Michael explained, *"Little One, your world has learned from each of its previous attempts. The shift takes place within the One Soul of Earth, and that requires that each individualized life consciousness is in agreement and alignment with the decision to change the Divine Purpose of Earth. The Paradigm Shift occurred when the final individualized energy of Earth said, 'I am complete in my experience of fear, I am ready.'*

"Many humans believe that God and other spiritual realms are making these decisions, but be assured it is the physical world that has decided to expand into Divine Love! Every life consciousness on Earth will change its Divine Purpose in this lifetime. NO ONE WILL BE LEFT BEHIND!

"The paradigm shift is the result of more and more Divine Love being expressed on the planet. Humanity brilliantly concluded that if each person on Earth continued to express the same amount of love as in previous incarnations, you would need more people expressing love to raise the vibratory frequency.

"Therefore, over the last century, you have greatly increased the human population of the Earth. Congratulations, you succeeded! The

paradigm shift is a done deal!" Michael was beginning to sound like my mother.

"The last time the Earth attempted this shift, a group of humans became impatient and tried to pull the Angelic energy into the Earth plane too rapidly, which tore the tectonic plates of the Earth apart."

"You told me about this at Agnes Vaille Falls; won't the doorways protect the Earth from repeating this problem?"

"They are one step in the process, but they will not be enough. In order to maintain the proper density of your planet as the vibratory frequency begins to rapidly increase, the Earth will physically manifest the paradigm shift over a period of years. You have created a five-year plan from 2007-2012, in which approximately twenty percent of all life consciousness will move their focus from fear to love each year.

"The natural world and humanity must move in synchronicity. Each human will take six to twenty-four months to make their individual shift; you are among the first group to move." I wasn't sure if this was because I was spiritually ready or the Angelic Realm just wanted a highly trained volunteer, and as usual, Michael read my thoughts.

"Both. You are very impatient, and we need to be able to communicate with the human race on a moment-to-moment basis in order to support the process. The timing of an individual's shift has been made with Divine Love. Each individual has chosen when to move, according to the gifts they bring to the new world.

"While humans may assume that the first to move are more spiritually enlightened, this is not necessarily true. It is actually the last two levels that were chosen first. These are the individuals who are most connected to the physical Earth and carry the vibratory frequencies needed to heal and rebalance your natural world. They have volunteered to hold Mother Earth's denser energy through the first part of the shift, in essence holding the planet together.

"The members of the final two tiers also know that their gifts cannot be used as long as humanity remains disconnected from the One Soul of Earth. It may appear that the individuals in the last two tiers are totally oblivious to the shift, but in reality they are simply being protected by the process. If one chooses to stay in fear out of love, they will not be asked to suffer through it."

"So will the paradigm shift be completed in five years?"

"Everyone will step into their new Divine Purpose in the next five years. The physical manifestation of a new world of love will take much longer. It will take at least five generations to release and reverse the effects of fear on humanity, and then the true bliss of learning how to express Divine Love on Earth will truly begin. This will be the hardest thing your planet has ever done; fear will not give up without a fight!"

It didn't take me long to figure out that while the moment of the paradigm shift occurred with a whisper, manifesting the paradigm shift in the physical plane was about to become very loud and chaotic. "Where do I start, Michael?"

"You have already begun. Your new Divine Purpose requires that you shift your mind, body, and emotions in order to allow the higher energy of your Divine Love or spiritual essence to flow safely and freely through your physical being.

"Organic life forms have within their physical makeup genetic triggers that turn on their spiritual DNA when the physical Earth and their individual bodies reach a preset vibratory frequency. Humans often call this genetic material junk DNA, but it is one of your greatest treasures! You have carried this dormant information within you since the beginning of life on Earth.

"Not all of your dormant material will be activated at this time. There are many more steps ahead of you, but the DNA that is currently being activated will interact with your present genetic structures causing each individual to change from within.

"Your physical bodies will become both stronger and less dense

at the same time. The spiritual energy enters the physical plane at the atomic level and the space between your electrons, protons, and neutrons will actually expand to accommodate the increased flow of spiritual energy. The molecules, cells, and organs of your body will follow suit as the light of your love oozes out of every pore of your skin.

"In addition, the spiritual DNA will begin to turn on all of your spiritual gifts. Individuals will begin to open up their clairaudient, clairvoyant, clairsentient, telepathic, and empathic abilities over the next few years. The human race will begin to see, hear, feel, taste, and smell spiritual energy. In time the physical and spiritual senses will even begin to overlap, allowing each of you to experience your Spirit within as easily as your physical body, mind, and emotions.

"Once the spiritual DNA is triggered, the process is automatic. This process is not an evolution of mankind; it is an expansion of every life consciousness on Earth. You cannot force it, stop it, or mess it up. At times, you will endure strange sensations within your body, be forced to stop and nap through a physical healing, change your beliefs, and experience new levels and depths of emotions. It will be a solitary journey; no two life consciousnesses on Earth can make the shift together. You are not fixing, healing, or transforming your world. You are about to embark on the creation of a new world.

"Little One, it's time to quit your job and start your own business!"

chapter fifteen

Bubbling

Be careful what you ask for! For months I had been praying for something new and exciting, and once it arrived I wasn't at all sure what to do with it. I had been asking to earn a living by channeling Michael since the early 1990s and was always told by Michael that it was not possible. I had even attempted to start my own holistic business on several occasions without success, so the Universe can't blame me for being a bit skeptical at Michael's recent comments. I decided that it was time to voice my concerns to the Angelic Realm.

Over the last six months, I had discovered that when I opened the matrix in my home, I was able to stand in its doorway. This allowed me to place one foot in the Angelic Realm, interacting with the Angels, while keeping the other in the physical plane and my own human consciousness. This method of communication prevented me from melting into the oneness of the Angelic Realm but allowed me to ask questions from a human perspective and retain much more information following each session.

If ever there had been a time that I needed more information, this was it! I opened the matrix and immediately thanked Michael and Uriel for all the information and explanations they had given me about the recent paradigm shift. I then began to explain to them my human perception of this change.

"From Earth, this paradigm shift feels like all of humanity is traveling around the planet at two hundred miles an hour on one of our fancy bullet trains. People are eating, drinking, talking, resting, moving from car to car, meeting new friends, and playing all sorts of fear-based games. Then without warning, the engineer of the train is told that we are going the wrong way and slams on the brakes!

"The train immediately derails, and the cars near the front of the train begin flipping over in cornfields and cities, propelling many of the occupants out of the train while trapping others under seats and debris. The cars in the middle of the train slip the tracks, and while they remain upright, their occupants are extremely shaken. The cars at the back of the train come to an abrupt halt and the individuals in those cars continue what they are doing even as they ask, 'Why are we stopping?'

"Now, I see myself as a compassionate person who cares about everyone on the train, but according to Michael, I am in one of the first cars, and it appears to me that I am being asked to derail my life on Earth and I could get badly hurt!"

"Little One, that is a very accurate analogy of what is happening. You are very perceptive, but it is only partially correct. You have forgotten to take into account the role of the Angelic Realm in the situation—after all, the paradigm shift is the Angelic Movement."

I immediately began to see emergency teams of Angels surrounding and entering the train, and it appeared that there were at least five or more Angels for each person. Some of the Angels were providing first aid and comfort to the people sitting in the cornfields and on the streets of cities and towns as other Angels began pulling people out of the rubble. There were Angels literally flying people to hospitals and healing centers as others guided individuals to new transportation.

I even noticed a few Angels taking people home to the Angelic Realm. Near the back of the train, I observed a large number of Angels simply watching over those that were not yet ready to disembark the train.

It was chaotic, and at times frightening, as family members and friends searched for one another and their baggage. Yet while it was hard to watch and even harder to feel, I soon recognized that this was not a disaster. Through all of the chaos and fear, I could feel the loving energy of peace, hope, and security. All any individual had to do was desire water, food, a blanket, medicine, or comfort and it instantaneously appeared in front of them.

The derailment of the train had freed us from our journey with fear. It would take time to get everyone off the train and heal all the physical, emotional, and mental wounds, and even longer for each of us to find the correct path to follow, but no individual would make the journey alone. We may not always see them, but the Angels remain constantly at our sides.

I felt much better, but for some unknown reason, I had the overwhelming need to warn the Angels that we humans have a tendency to make things harder than they need to be. "We may not always listen to you, even when we know you're right."

I received a chorus of responses. *"Ah yes, rampant free will. That's to be expected. You never have before, why start now? That's a given. We are you, so you're really just not listening to yourselves. We expect nothing less. What fun would that be? It's the way of your world. We have infinite possibilities to deal with everything you could possibly ignore. We like surprises. Your planet is anything but boring. Let the fun begin!"*

These responses were accompanied by wave after wave of energy moving towards the bubble of our physical universe with a sense of play and joy that I had never experienced before. Truly, the Angelic Realm was elated with the shift on planet Earth. I felt like I was at a birthday party with a bunch of preschoolers who, after finishing off the cake and ice cream, had just discovered the piñata. It was just too sweet to resist, so I jumped into the Angelic Realm and melted into the party!

Two weeks later, I took another leap of faith and quit my job. That same week, I was doing readings at Celebration Conscious Living Store, and when I told the owner about my recent experiences, he offered me a part-time retail position in addition to my readings. The Angels really had heard my concerns, and this job brought many blessings beyond merely calming my fears of financial ruin.

The extra money was enough to pay my bills during those first few months, and I soon discovered that once I was available to my clients on a regular basis, my home business began to rapidly increase. In fact, Michael seemed to be sending people to me. I had numerous individuals tell me that they had received information in meditation to come and see me or that they had been wanting a reading and had suddenly come across my website for the first time.

Within four months, my readings were paying all of my bills. There was rarely any extra, but I was happier than I had ever been. The impossible had become possible, and I was finally making a living doing what I loved most in my life. My leap of faith had been physically validated by Michael and the Angelic Realm.

My job at Celebration brought another blessing. For the first time in my life, I was presenting all of me to the outer world. Everyone that walked into the store was aware that I channeled an Angel. I no longer had to ignore or hide that part of myself from my co-workers and customers. In fact, in this environment my spiritual gifts were an asset that I could use to help anyone who asked.

Michael actually came to work with me every day, and it was refreshing and fun to be able to express both of us to the world without the fear of being censored or possibly even fired. However, the more I opened up to others, the more aware I became of how people were reacting to our energies.

Most people loved the softness of Michael's energy and wanted to melt into it, but there were others that actually seemed to get a little uneasy, hyper, and even agitated by our presence. These individuals appeared to be drawn to the energy and afraid of it at the same time. So one night after work, I asked Michael what was happening.

"Little One, it is not my energy that triggers fear, it is yours. You have stepped into the new paradigm and carry its energy in your body. The DNA within each organic organism is designed to activate their individual process, allowing the energy of the Angelic Realm to move through the individual from the inside out, slowly and gently pushing all fear out of the body at a rate that can do no harm. However, touching another individual who carries the higher energy of the Angelic Movement can also begin the awakening process.

"When individuals are prematurely triggered in this way, two things can combine to create unnecessary discomfort. The first is that individuals immediately recognize and want this new energy and mistakenly believe they must release all their fears in order to receive it. This belief can cause a sudden release of fear, which overloads their minds, bodies and emotions and actually inhibits the release process.

"Simultaneously, humans are attracting what they want from the world around them by pulling energy towards them, further trapping the very fear they are trying to release from within their bodies and auric fields. Any fear that is stuck in one's energy is experienced over and over until it is released."

"Why does my energy trigger fear when yours does not?"

"Our energy is pure Angelic energy and contains only the vibratory frequency of love. This vibratory frequency is the same in all life consciousness on Earth. When humans feel our energy, they feel the pure love of their own soul essence.

"Your energy, like all individualized energies of the Earth plane, has a unique range of vibratory frequencies which contains both love and fear. The love you express triggers the needs and desires of

Divine Love in others, but at the same time your fears also activate their fears."

"If my shift into the new paradigm will take six to twenty-four months, what can I do in the meantime to stop frightening people?"

"It is not about your individual process. Fear is a part of Earth and will continue as long as the planet exists. You need fear to survive the physicality of your planet. Without it, you are in danger of jumping off a building because you think you can fly or being eaten by a bear or hit by a bus. Fear is a tool that will help keep you safe."

"So what can I do?"

"You can Bubble."

"I've been protecting myself with energy bubbles for years, Michael."

"The bubbles you have learned to utilize in the past were designed to protect you by reflecting the fears of the outer world back to their source. We are proposing that you allow the love within you to flow outward to every life consciousness you touch on the planet. This bubble is created by your soul essence rather than your physical energy.

"Your spiritual DNA is altering your etheric field as well as your denser physical being and is currently opening your ascending heart chakra. There are a few humans who have opened this chakra in the past, but every individual on Earth will start using this chakra within the next few years. The ascending heart chakra is in the center of your chest between the heart and throat chakras and lies directly above the thymus gland.

"This energy center is connected directly to the Angelic Realm. In simple terms, this energy is the vibratory frequency of your soul essence and is untouched and unaltered by the lower energies of fear currently held within your body, mind, and emotions. Are you ready to receive this energy?"

"Yes!"

"Relax and take three deep breaths. Now we want you to visualize

a door in your ascending heart. Don't worry if you can't see it. We know you are not very visual; just use your imagination." I immediately saw a medieval castle door. *"Open the door, look inside, and tell me what you see."*

"Swirling gold energy."

"This is your doorway between the Angelic and physical realms. Angelic energy is non-intrusive; you must invite it in. We ask you to invite the energy to flow through your body and create a bubble of energy around you so that you are literally sitting inside your own Angelic energy."

This sounded like a personal mini-matrix, so I invited the energy to enter my world, and it immediately began to form a large bubble about twelve inches outside of my body. As it began to flow, it started to change color and Michael told me not to worry about it—whatever color I needed would automatically flow from Spirit.

"Little One, you will need to consciously create this bubble three times a day for the next thirty days. It will become denser with each invitation into your being, and while its flow will become automatic after that time period, you can greatly increase your expression of love to the world by choosing each day to do so. Add this request to your five-minute meditations and your life will change immensely.

"As the bubble becomes thicker, its outer edge will become the energy you offer to the world. It will also allow you to both feel and experience your own fear from a place of safety and prevent you from imposing your fears on others. The flow of Angelic love is the highest vibratory frequency and most powerful energy on Earth.

"You will soon find that as your energy flows from the center of your being outward, any love that flows towards you will simply melt into your being, and lower energies will begin to dissolve upon contact with your bubble. Fear can no longer dilute love, and there is no need to be protected from love."

Bubbling was the first expression of Divine Love in the physical plane that Michael taught me. After the first few months, I began to feel the love of my own Angelic energy on my skin, especially when I was naked or in water. The softness and sensuality of this energy dissolved much of the harshness that had previously monopolized my life and made it much easier for me to deal with my own negativity.

The only consistent problem I have with my bubble is that I like to match my outfits to my morning bubble. Unfortunately, by lunch, my energy has often shifted and I am no longer color-coordinated. So much for the colors of my soul!

I must admit that for the first six months, I subconsciously continued to use bubbling to protect myself, until one night when I was in a restaurant next to a family with a very fussy baby. I was tired and didn't want to deal with the baby's discomfort, so I quickly reinforced my bubble. The baby immediately stopped fussing and looked directly at me. Then he began to laugh as he pulled the brightest pink and yellow bubble I had ever seen right out of the center of his ascending heart.

Now I think baby laughter is the greatest sound on Earth, but this baby's laugh topped them all. It was loud, exuberant, joyous, and contagious. No one in the building was immune, and by the time the baby had exhausted himself, we had all shared a joyous moment of oneness.

I don't remember what I had for dinner that night, but it was the best meal I have ever had. Michael taught me the technique of bubbling, but it took a baby to teach me how to truly share love through bubbling.

chapter sixteen

A New Journey

"Wake up Little One, we need you to go the post office this morning and apply for a passport."

I excitedly jumped out of bed, got dressed, gathered the necessary documents, and asked Michael, "Where are we going?"

"The post office."

I have never quite figured out if God and the Angels really enjoy testing me or if they are just singularly focused at times. Whichever it is, I have learned to silently go with the flow and ask questions later. In this case, it took about an hour to drive to the post office, complete the application, and get back in the car.

"Little one, you have a new soul essence entering your physical body and it's time to create your second matrix."

I was caught completely off guard! I had never considered the possibility that my DNA and physical body were capable of such an act. However, my further questions went unanswered as Michael became very mysterious about my new soul essence and the timing and placement of the second doorway. Finally, I just couldn't stand it anymore and asked for a hint. Michael immediately showed me three small palm trees, nothing more, just three small palm trees.

I was beginning to suspect that Divine timing was again playing a huge role in my life, so I dealt with my frustration in the usual manner—I changed the color of my hair. I became a redhead for the first time in my life. It was the end of March, and I had originally bargained with Spirit to give my relationship with Pink Lady one year. My birthday was a few weeks away and changing my hair color was my way of extending our contract.

Michael seemed to recognize my commitment and finally explained, *"Little One, your body is now capable of creating six matrixes. Your Divine Path is to open doorways on six different continents between now and the end of 2012. The next doorway will be placed in the British Isles during October's new moon. This matrix will be predominately orange in color and your Orange soul essence plans to enter your physical body on your birthday and begin its creation."*

On my fifty-sixth birthday, I entered Sacred Space and was met by Pink Lady and Green Guy. Blue was sitting on top of a mountain and Purple was hanging out at the mouth of a new cave, as elusive as ever. Pink Lady informed me it was not yet time to deal with Purple, so I looked for Big Bud. The moment my mind turned to Buddy, I saw him loping across the valley with an enormous male archer riding on his back. Evidently Buddy already knew Orange!

Orange was carrying a bow and had a pouch filled with arrows strapped to his back. His skin was an intense orange, and his energy seemed to radiate out of his body like sunbursts. His smooth leather clothes and suede boots were also orange, and as he jumped off Buddy, he looked at me with intense golden eyes but said nothing. I was about to learn that Orange does not speak; Orange is the energy of pure manifestation!

Pink Lady explained, *"The essence of Orange emanates from the part of the Angelic Realm humans know as the void. This area of the Angelic Realm contains the infinity of all that is yet to be manifested and experienced. Orange is joining us to anchor the FINN energy, which has never existed on the planet before, into the physical core of the Earth. While the human Viki Hart will experience this energy, it is the children soon to be born into the new paradigm that will understand how to utilize this energy."*

The memory of the Rock Lady of Arizona telling me to return to Colorado because the new children would be looking for me there flooded my mind as I surrendered to the power of my human connection with this new soul essence.

I closed my eyes, leaned into my Archer and immediately saw an orange ray explode out of the depths of the void's blackness and enter my ascending heart chakra. In contrast to this intense burst of color, our joining brought into my being a silent stillness that immediately calmed my body, mind, and emotions, and suspended me in time and space. This new essence knew nothing of Earth's fear! The energy of Orange was indeed the pure manifestation of a new physical expression of Divine Love on Earth.

As Orange integrated into my physical being over the next few months, I began to receive information and visions about the new doorway. I saw a waterfall surrounded by lush green trees, grasses, ferns, and other plants and flowers that felt as old as time itself.

At one point, I saw myself walk across a bridge with a metal railing and start down a trail filled with dancing fairies. At other times, I was shown the outline of two people standing at a bend in the trail, a bald-headed man surrounded by a gold light, and a Victorian bedroom.

Still, I had no idea where in the British Isles I was going. My father's family came from Scotland (Lockhart/Stuart). I have always felt a kinship with the Druid beliefs, and I have always wanted to visit Ireland, so I was ready for anything. However, Michael continued to be of very little help in my search. He even seemed to revel in my search to solve this mystery and answered each of my questions with, *"Little One, the answers lie within your own DNA."*

I finally realized that if the information was within my body, I should be able to muscle test for the answer. On my next visit to see my friend Marsha Sterling for a reading and Jin Shin session, we started asking questions. Sure enough, my body was able to tell me that my destination was the one place I had not considered, Wales.

I rushed home after my appointment and searched waterfalls of Wales on the computer. There are a lot of waterfalls in Wales, all of them incredibly beautiful. I went through them one by one until my vision appeared on the screen in front of me. I was going to open a doorway at Melincourt Falls in the county of Neath, Wales.

Once I discovered the site of the doorway, Michael became more helpful in my preparation. Michael seemed to have the ability of at least partially controlling what Internet sites I ended up on. Within a few short weeks, I had paid for airline tickets to London, bus tickets to Wales, and a room in an old Victorian bed and breakfast. I bought British pounds for spending money and completed all these tasks just a week before the bottom dropped out of the US dollar. I quickly learned that while I was not making much money channeling Angels, they consistently offered me both perfect timing and information on where to find all the best deals!

By early July, I had completed all my worldly preparations for my trip and began looking inward. I had discovered the musical group Celtic Woman in December of 2006 through their PBS special "A New Journey," and I immediately began using two songs from their CD to open and close the temporary doorway in my home. Now their music accompanied all of my aerobic and strength training, and by the end of the summer, I truly felt I was on a new journey.

This would be my first solitary trip out of the United States, and I was more than a little apprehensive. I must admit that there were times when I doubted my ability to complete this task, but something inside me just kept pushing me forward. Looking back, I now know that I was being led by an Angel and my own DNA into a new level of trust and spiritual awareness, and nothing in this physical world could have stopped me.

The physical process of creating the matrix within my body was much the same as that of Agnes Vaille Falls. I was required to set intentions, strengthen my body, and then bring my mind and emotions into alignment. You would think that the second time around would be easier, right?

Wrong! My intentions for this doorway were entirely different than those of the first, and it was like starting all over again. By mid-July, Michael had connected my energy into Melincourt Falls, and I could feel the very soul of the planet flowing towards me from this magical place. I knew that this doorway was my gift to Mother Earth and that I would reconnect with her through this journey.

For decades, I had ignored this planet as I struggled to find a way to rescue my soul and leave. During this time, I had been taught over and over again that Mother Earth is simply a lifeless resource that, depending on your point of view, needs to be managed, exploited, or protected by humanity.

All of those thoughts and emotions now had to be stripped away. It was a painful and hectic few weeks, but by the first of September, I understood that Mother Earth and I were one, and I was ready to open to the full power of her loving consciousness and embrace my life on Earth as both a blessing and a miracle.

Just as I thought everything was ready for my trip, Michael suggested that I ask for a gift from the Angelic Realm for opening the doorway. I had always been uncomfortable asking for gifts, so this suggestion was rather perplexing for me. I had no idea what kind of gifts the Angelic Realm had to offer in this type of situation, and could not think of anything that I felt worthy of asking for.

Then one afternoon, while doing a phone reading for my friend Suz, I felt Orange's familiar energy of silent stillness emanating from her body. Suz was just a few weeks pregnant, and the energy was coming from her unborn child! I knew instantly that the gift that I wanted from the Angelic Realm was to be able to let as many people as possible experience this energy.

As soon as I got off the phone, I asked Michael if this was possible. *"We were hoping you would ask, Little One. Yes, it is possible. Suz's child is one of the first children of the new paradigm to bring this energy to Earth. You will need his help—"*

"It's a boy!"

"Yes, it's a boy, and you will need his help to create a tool that will allow you to both open and close a temporary matrix that can surround large numbers of people. Currently, when you open a doorway, one or two other individuals can plug into it through your energy field, and that is safe for short periods of time. However, you need a method of sealing the doorway and separating yourself from the energies of others in order to safely hold the door open for larger groups and longer periods of time. Suz's son has offered to help you set up a physical energy grid in the new matrix, which we will activate within you the night before you open the doorway."

"Does Suz have to go to Wales with me?"

"No, this can be done by piggy-backing the child's energy onto one of Suz's long-distance Reiki treatments. We will use seven Ogham symbols, one in each of your main chakras to create the grid. The child will send his FINN energy through the symbols across the physical plane as Orange matches it from within your body creating the grid.

"The following morning, you will activate the grid and open the matrix at the falls. After opening the doorway and completing the ritual, you will use the symbols to close and seal the grid. Once you have done this, the grid will automatically activate every time you open a temporary doorway, and you will then be able to safely close and seal it upon completion of your ritual."

Michael gave me the seven symbols and their positions in the grid, and I sent them to Suz, who already knew she was having a boy. My dear friend didn't even question the sanity of putting her unborn child to work making an energy grid as we set up a long distance Reiki healing and grid delivery system for the following month.

Eight months later, on May 21, 2008, Finnigan Corbett Pittman entered the world at a whopping eight pounds, twelve ounces.

chapter seventeen

My Very Own Magical Bubble!

"A dream is a wish your heart makes when you're fast asleep," are the first song lyrics I remember singing as a child. I'm sure I heard other songs before this one, but the music and words of this song remain forever etched in my human psyche.

Of course, a few other things also stuck with me from the movie *Cinderella,* such as Fairy Godmothers are good, stepmothers are bad, and in order to be successful and happy in life you must meet your Prince Charming and live happily ever after. As I have gotten older, I have discovered that Fairy Godmothers and Angels really are good, blended families can be wonderful but take a lot of work, and a Prince passes gas just like all the other guys.

Even with the knowledge that this movie might have been slightly deceptive, the idea that a dream is a wish your heart makes when you're fast asleep still intrigues me. I have very vivid nighttime dreams in full cinematic color, and love the crazy way my dreams flow.

Through the years, I have come to recognize the different types and meanings of many of my dreams. There are those dreams that are simply a rehashing of the day or even a movie or television show that I have recently watched. These dreams allow me to release thoughts and emotions that I had hidden away during the experience or perhaps even take the leading role in someone else's fantasy. I find this process both fun and refreshing.

There are also the dreams that allow my fears to come to the surface, which include both the discomfort of being naked in front of large groups of people and my nightmares of being physically threatened. Like most people, I do not like these types of dreams, but I trust that they have some purpose in my life. Since I have not had any nightmares (at least that I remember) in years, I accept the process as a necessary part of being human.

However, it is my lucid dreams that I truly adore. I define lucid dreams as my physical brain's interpretation of real spiritual experiences that take place while I'm sleeping. These include my flying dreams, my sensation of true bliss after awaking from a night in the Angelic Realm, and my activities as I astral project around the planet. Michael has told me for years that all humans do spiritual work while sleeping—after all, the Spirit does not need to sleep so why would it want to waste one single moment of its Earth incarnation. So I was not surprised when my lucid dreaming began to greatly increase in the weeks preceding my trip to the British Isles. I knew that my mind was aligning with my spiritual journey.

At the same time, Michael asked me to start spending some of my time on the exercise machine daydreaming about my trip. *"Daydreams connect the Spirit directly to your emotions. We want you to add as much wonder, awe, and joy as possible to your trip. Both lucid dreams and daydreams act as an emotional catalyst for physical manifestation on your planet."* Perhaps if more humans understood how productive dreaming can be, there would be less sleep deprivation and more conscious manifestation in our culture.

I was also experiencing an increase in visions during my meditations and was having difficulty interpreting them. *"Little One, unlike lucid dreams and daydreams which deal with energy that is currently undergoing physical manifestation or experience on your planet, visions are opportunities yet to be chosen for manifestation on the Earth plane. Dreams are physically created within the human mind while visions are offerings of the Spirit.*

"When the human mind confuses the two, it creates expectations of what is happening, what will happen, or creates ideas about what you are supposed to do to make something happen. If you choose a vision and allow it to melt into your thoughts and emotions, you can create it. But if you focus solely on the vision, the energy will not take physical form."

I understood what Michael was saying to me, but I had no idea why he was telling me this now. *"We want you to drop all your expectations about the trip. It was necessary to use your mind to create the trip by getting a passport, making the necessary reservations, and taking care of your financial needs, but it is now time to allow Spirit to take over. You have dreamed of visiting the British Isles all your life, and you have a vision of the new matrix and doorway. Live your dream and do not let your mind try to force your visions into the confines and limitations of its expectations. Allow yourself to expand into each new moment and experience it as it comes. Expect nothing and experience all!"*

A week later, I dropped Buddy off at the kennel, put my suitcases in the car, and did a final meditation before leaving for the airport. I ended my meditation with the request to expect nothing and experience all! Immediately, I felt an energy shift, both within my physical being and around me.

My mind, which had been racing with last minute preparations, calmed, and a warm sense of serenity swept through my emotions as my body relaxed into a state of total comfort and joy. I felt Michael's full presence next to me and knew I was walking with Angels, perceiving my world with love, and being guided by my own pure spiritual instinct. My journey had begun!

It was as if I was moving in my very own magical bubble that the outside world could no longer affect. I could see only beauty and joy in the mountains and foothills around me. I flowed around traffic with ease and even though I had never driven to the Denver Airport before, I knew exactly where I was going and the easiest route to get there. Once I entered the airport, I automatically choose the quickest check-in and security lines and was at my gate within fifteen minutes of my arrival. Then the fun began!

I had over three hours before my flight left, so I did the two things I love to do most at airports—eat and watch people. I have always liked to look at people's outfits and try to figure out where they have been or where they are going, and then I fantasize about what it would be like to be there. However, on this trip I was just so delighted with where I was going that I spent most of my time feeling sorry for everyone departing for a different destination. I secretly knew that my trip was going to be the best trip ever taken by anyone who had flown out of Denver International Airport!

I was correct! The plane left on time, we had a great dinner, the person in the seat next to me had a great sense of humor, I slept well, breakfast was great, and I was awed by the English countryside as we flew into Heathrow. I even woke up once during the night and felt Michael next to me and asked him why he was sitting outside of the window instead of inside. He said he thinks the seats are too small, and it seems he really can fly.

I loved the energy of England from the moment I stepped off the plane. The English are very civil, and my magical bubble allowed me to quickly breeze through customs, pick up my bags, and even grab a sandwich and chocolate bar before boarding the bus to Wales.

As I relaxed on the bus, jet lag decided to make an appearance, and I had no choice but to take a nap. Several hours later, I almost jumped out of my seat without any idea of what had awakened me. There weren't many people on the bus and everyone around me appeared calm, so I sat back and looked out the window.

We were crossing a long bridge that separated England and Wales, and I could see the ocean off to my left. Michael immediately said, *"You're home, Little One,"* and I could feel the energy of the Wales matrix surround me as the bus reached the land. This sensation reminded me of the moment I first saw Pikes Peak in the distance and felt that I had come home for the first time, yet this was a very different energy. I felt my whole body soften, and I intuitively knew that within the infinite colors of my soul, I had lived and died in this place many times before.

For a moment, I wondered if this journey was a significant part of a larger Divine Plan and then realized it didn't matter. I was here now in this moment and that was all that I wanted or cared about. Well, that and chocolate. I suddenly realized I was hungry. We stopped in Cardiff and a number of small towns on the way to Port Talbot, and after a short cab ride I arrived in Briton Ferry shortly after dark and was led to the Victorian bedroom seen in my earlier vision. I was physically exhausted and after eating a light dinner, collapsed into bed.

The next morning I was rested, alert, and ready to go. After a wonderful breakfast and a few directions from the hostess of my Bed and Breakfast, I caught the bus and headed for the town of Melincourt. I was still in my magical bubble! Within the bustle of the morning rush, I automatically walked directly to the correct gate at the bus station, and everywhere I went, people treated me like an old friend. There were even individuals that asked me directions and then laughed when I started talking and they realized that I was not from Wales.

When the bus got to Melincourt, the driver directed me to the falls. The bus stop was beyond the trailhead, and I found myself having to walk back down the hill and across a bridge with a metal railing to reach it.

The trail was both beautiful and energetically amazing. The path and stream occupied the narrow space between two gently sloping canyon walls, which were covered with massive trees, ferns, grasses, and flowers that stretched out to reach every ray of sunlight that found its way to the canyon floor. The moment I stepped into the canyon, I felt transported back in time to the primal beginnings of Mother Earth. This place was not of man, but of Mother Earth in her purest form and I was honored to be an invited guest.

I paused to express my gratitude and thanksgiving for the opportunity that I was being given and was immediately greeted by a host of dancing fairies and other entities. I could easily feel the presence of Angels, fairies, and a host of creatures from other realms, but it was rare for me to actually see them. However, this seemed to be a grand exception and I was delighted to not only see them, but to communicate with them as well.

The fairies knew why I was there and appeared to be very excited about the doorway. They asked me questions about how I was going to open the doorway and pointed out their favorite plants and rocks along the trail. They shared a wealth of information with me about their home and seemed disappointed to find out that I was not opening the doorway until the next day. These fairies lived in the moment and seemed to think that planning ahead had little or no value.

We had been dancing our way down the trail for about fifteen minutes when I heard the roar of water and came around a large bend and saw the falls for the first time. It had been raining the last few days, and Melincourt Falls was flowing in all its glory. There was so much water that there was even a second waterfall off to one side. The grandeur of the falls took my breath away. It towered eighty feet above me, and its lush surroundings created a rich contrast to the barren rocks of Agnes Vaille Falls. I felt my mind, body, and emotions surrender to an ancient memory of my human oneness with Mother Earth. This matrix truly was to be my gift and expression of Divine Love to my planet, and this magical place was ready to receive it!

I left the falls, reassuring the fairies I would be back the next morning, and caught the bus back to the Neath station. I knew that I needed a crystal for the ritual and asked Michael where to find it. He guided me down several streets and into an enclosed market place where I was immediately sidetracked by a sandwich shop.

After satisfying my physical needs, I wandered into a crystal shop at the back of the market and found the perfect crystal. The owner, Peter Harris, who just happened to be the bald-headed man from my visions and said he channeled Archangel Gabrielle, patiently listened to all my plans about opening an Angelic Doorway in his neighborhood and then generously shared his life's purpose with me.

I returned to Briton Ferry feeling both happy and overwhelmed. One by one, my visions were physically manifesting before my eyes. In my heart, I was sure of every step I was taking and felt a calm sense of total fulfillment. Yet in my mind, there was a nagging voice that said this was too easy and could not actually be happening. Surely I was about to wake up from this magical dream. I needed to physically relax and allow my mind to calm itself so I went for a walk in the park.

Jersey Park is beautiful! It is filled with benches scattered among tree lined paths, picnic tables, flower beds, formal gardens, a bridge and waterway system, and a children's playground. Thirty minutes later, I was still feeling a little dazed so I sat down on a bench, closed my eyes, and asked Michael for a little validation. Was it really possible that I had traveled across the continental United States and the Atlantic Ocean to find exactly the right waterfall in the right place to open an Angelic Doorway, or was I just crazy?

Michael's answer was soft and gentle, *The answer is right in front of you.* I opened my eyes, and in the formal garden directly in front of me were three small palm trees.

chapter eighteen

Melincourt Falls

A mind is a terrible thing to waste, but quite frankly it's a wonderful thing to turn off every now and then. I don't know if it was the jet lag, the people stepping out of my visions into the physical world, or the three small palm trees, but my mind finally gave up trying to make sense of it all and began to merely experience what was in front of me in each moment. This act of letting go actually increased the magic within my bubble by intensifying both my physical and spiritual senses.

As my vision, hearing, taste, and touch all instantly became more acute, my spiritual awareness of the energy of the people, plants, and animals increased as well. I became aware of the physical condition of those around me when I tuned into my own heartbeat and breathing. When I focused on my emotions, I began to feel the joys and sadness in others. Somehow turning off my mind allowed me to connect in oneness with the world around me, yet I was not overwhelmed as I had been prior to turning off my empathic abilities.

In fact, this connection was comforting. I felt safe and secure as if the people, animals, plants, and all of Wales were wrapping me in a warm blanket of pure love. I knew the matrix within me was starting to activate. The ritual was about to begin!

I ate dinner, returned to my room, and got ready for bed. My friend, Suz and I had set the long distance healing for ten o'clock in the evening, and Michael suggested I lay down to receive the FINN energy grid. Suz's Reiki was amazingly warm and soft, and I immediately relaxed into a light meditation and reached out for Michael.

However, Michael did not reach back, and I suddenly felt a cramping in my lower abdomen that was so severe I pulled my legs up and went into a fetal position. *"It's okay, Little One, ask to open to the grid and slowly breathe each symbol into its chakra."* I followed Michael's instructions and the pain began to lessen and then disappeared completely. The warm softness of the Reiki energy returned to completely fill my entire body, and as Michael wrapped his energy around me, I fell asleep.

I awoke the next morning feeling surprisingly energetic and hungry. There was no weakness or lack of balance as there had been in Colorado. In fact, I felt a new fullness in the core of my body and thought I might have actually gained weight overnight. *"Don't worry, Little One, it's energetic, not physical, and you need to eat a big breakfast."* I love to eat for the cause; the total lack of guilt over calories just seems to make everything taste better!

After eating everything on the menu, I caught the bus to Melincourt and arrived at the trailhead shortly before ten in the morning. The fairies were there to greet me and excitedly accompanied me down the path to the base of the waterfall. Then suddenly they were gone, and I was left alone to complete the ritual.

I began by asking permission of the Angelic Realm to open a doorway, and as before, I heard the infinite echoes of thank you flowing through me. However, this time I simply opened my heart and let the energy flow through every atom of my being. In the fifteen months since the opening at Agnes Vaille Falls, I had learned how to receive love and it was joyous! I then placed my palms upon the ground and asked permission of Mother Earth to place a doorway at this site.

Instantly, the grid within me activated, and I connected into oneness with Mother Earth. I was aware of her massive consciousness, which seemed to dwarf my limited human mind. More than that, though, I suddenly felt her physical body become my body, her emotions flowing through my emotions.

I could not breathe or move any part of my body and found myself lying on the ground paralyzed by pain. I could feel all the physical pain that Mother Earth was experiencing as humanity crushed her bones into gravel and dug into her body to remove the fossil fuels and minerals that nurtured her physical being. I struggled to survive on contaminated air that was no longer being filtered by primal forests, and felt the clogging of her arteries as her rivers were dammed and miles of trash was dumped in her oceans. I shared her longing for all the plants and animals that have been pushed to extinction by the carelessness and disrespect of humanity, but most of all, I felt painful intense hunger. Mother Earth was starving for humanity's love!

My mind flashed back to the moment of my surgery at age thirteen when Purple left my body, flowed into the ground, and joined in oneness with Mother Earth. I finally understood that my years of anorexia and obsessive need to rescue and save Purple had merely been reflections of my relationship with this planet. I was stunned and overwhelmed with guilt. I had withheld love from my planet in the mistaken belief that I could only be made whole again by some unknown Spirit from another realm.

For the first time, I realized that my wholeness lies in the love shared by Purple, the Viki I now am, and Mother Earth, for we all emanate from the one source. We are one, and what happens to one part of us happens to every part of us. In that moment of clarity, I chose love and heard my voice cry out over the roar of the falls, "I will save you. Somehow, I will find a way to save us." Instantly, my pain stopped, as a flow of gentle warmth entered my body from the ground below me, and I felt the hunger within begin to lessen.

A few minutes later, I sat up, reached into the cool water cascading down the canyon wall, and allowed its spray to wash away my tears. I then took my place on a rock a few yards away and began to set my intentions. The moment I released the matrix from my body, it appeared all around me. It was staggering, at least twice the size of the Colorado cylinder, with intense bright orange walls that appeared almost solid. I was mesmerized by its beauty and the softness of its energy, and for the first few minutes of its existence it sang in a sweet high-pitched tone that reminded me of a wind chime. It was hard for me to realize that energy this soft could actually exist on Earth. It felt more like the energy of the veil between the physical and Angelic Realms, and I wondered if this was what our primal Earth felt like before the introduction of fear.

"Little One, look up!"

As I looked up at the top of the falls, I saw the doorway open. The white light was so bright that I had to close my eyes for a moment. When I opened them, white energy from the Angelic Realm was pouring down the falls and filling the matrix from the ground up. The water in the falls appeared to be flowing in slow motion, and I could see the white light flow into individual drops of water and was able to watch each drop as it slid over the rocks, into the stream, and began to move out of the canyon. *"Little One, each drop of water, and the Angelic energy within it, will reach the ocean in a few short days. Mother Earth will use it to heal her oceans as well as her land."*

I felt a sudden surge of hope rise from deep within me and realized that even with all the spiritual knowledge that I had gained over the last few years, I had not believed that Mother Earth could be saved from humanity's greed. However, the immense power of light and love that I saw in just one drop of water showed me that it is not humanity that will save our planet, it is Mother Earth that will save humanity. I walked into this ritual believing that Mother Earth was starving for humanity's love and walked away knowing I had it backwards. It is humanity that hungers to reconnect with Mother Earth and the Angelic Realm.

"Little One, you have given a great gift to Mother Earth. You have opened your heart and reconnected with your planet, and your human heart is finally home. Thousands of years from now, Angels will be able to walk through this doorway and interact with humans as easily as humans interact with each other. Perhaps you will be one of the first Angels to do so."

I did not step through the doorway into the Angelic Realm at Melincourt Falls. Instead, I invited the Angels to join me here on Earth for a little while, and I was able to see them with the awe and wonder of a child. The fairies joined in the party, and for almost an hour on October 11, 2007, at the site of Melincourt Falls, the natural world, a bunch of fairies and Angels, and one human melted into the laughter and joy of oneness.

"Little One, it's time to close the grid." I reluctantly pulled out my crystal, set my intent, and drew the Ogham symbols into each of my chakras. Immediately the walls of the matrix, the flow of energy through the doorway, and the Angels disappeared from my sight, and I knew it was time to go.

As I picked up my backpack, a couple came around the bend in the trail and we started talking. They lived in the area and hiked around the falls quite often. We talked for a long time and then hiked to the top of the falls before they offered me a ride back to Neath. They were the last two people from my visions, and I thanked Michael for sending them to take care of me after I opened the matrix. I did find their presence very grounding, and with their help, I avoided harming my physical body in the hours following my ritual.

I remained in Wales for a few more days, visiting Neath Abby, watching a sunset over the Atlantic Ocean, exploring Swansea Bay, shopping, hiking, and doing several readings for people I met along the way. I didn't want to leave. Michael was right; I was finally home.

In less than a week, I had come to know many of the people that I met on the street, in the post office, grocery store, restaurants, and Jersey Park by name. Wherever I went, the Welsh people looked into my eyes as they spoke and took the time to really see who I was as a human as they listened to the song of my Spirit. For the first time in many years, I felt embraced by love, connected to a tribe, and physically, mentally, and emotionally taken care of on the Earth plane.

I resisted leaving and hoped that the hour delay of the departure of my bus back to England and the unexpected need to change terminals at Heathrow were signs that I needed to move to Wales. Unfortunately, Michael assured me that it was not time for this change in my lifestyle, but he did leave the door open to this possibility in the future.

My time at Heathrow Airport and on the plane turned into a real party, and I quickly learned that while the English, Scottish, and Irish shared some very interesting antagonisms with each other, they all agreed that the Welsh are wonderfully polite, kind, and open. My final lesson of the trip was that the Welsh have no fear of love; the people of this small country simply open their hearts and embrace everyone and everything around them. I realized that a new world of love was now possible. The people of Wales had already created a model for us to use, and even if I could not live with them, I could learn to live like them.

I arrived home to find myself extremely jet lagged. Several of my friends suggested sitting outside with my back to the sun, returning to my normal schedule, and eating or drinking a variety of different substances to readjust. I thanked them, but I didn't do any of those things because I didn't want to adjust. I wanted to wake up in my bed and for a moment feel like I could walk out my front door and be on the streets of Briton Ferry. I needed to hold onto the energy of the Wales matrix for as long as possible.

Finally, Michael suggested I open the matrix in my home. I

opened the back door and let Buddy go out on the deck, placed my crystals in a sacred circle, put "The Voice" on, and began my ritual. Immediately, Buddy charged into the house with his ears almost straight up and lay down in the circle. I continued opening the matrix and by the time I was done, Buddy was lying on his back with his feet in the air and his tongue hanging out. He looked a little stoned. I lay down in the circle with him and soaked in the energy for a while before asking Michael what was happening.

"Little One, the energies of the two matrixes have blended within you, and Buddy loves it. The Wales matrix has softened the energy, changed its sound, and reduced the change it causes in barometric pressure so it is no longer uncomfortable for him. Look out the window."

In the tree just outside my living room window were two squirrels sitting perfectly still as they stared into the house. In the branches near them were three large crows shifting back and forth from one foot to the other as they faced the window. "Michael, the birds seem to be dancing to their own music."

"They're dancing to the rhythms of the matrix." The squirrels and birds continued this amusing behavior until I closed the matrix. They went on their way, and I have not seen this behavior since. However, Buddy continued to join me inside the circle each time I opened it.

The following weekend, my body returned to Colorado time, and Buddy and I drove to Agnes Vaille Falls. It was late October, but there were still quite a few bright twinkling yellow leaves on the aspens in the canyon. I said a silent prayer of gratitude for the beauty of Mother Earth. My trip to Wales had left me with the magical ability to feel the beauty of our planet deep within me, and I felt the presence of so many plants and rocks that I had never noticed before.

As I walked into the entrance of the upper canyon, I suddenly felt the energy of the Wales matrix! I closed my eyes, and in my mind I saw its intense orange energy just before me. We were several hundred yards away from the boundary of the original doorway, yet the energy of both doorways seemed to flow in and out of each other. As I proceeded up the mountain, I could feel the original boundary and a subtle shift as the Agnes Vaille energy took center stage. I was overwhelmed; the energy field was almost three times larger than the last time I had been there!

"Little One, you create the matrixes within your body, each matrix being larger in size to fit over the outside boundary of the previous matrix. What is created within you is also created outside of you. You did not just open the orange matrix in Wales, you opened the energy of Agnes Vaille Falls within that space as well. In that moment, the Wales matrix was added to the original doorway here in Colorado. It is time for you to accept that every inch of this planet is your home and open yourself to all the love that Mother Earth has to offer."

As I reached into the falling water, I opened my heart fully to Mother Earth and embraced my connection with this beautiful planet. I felt totally at home as I saw my life on Earth suddenly stretch itself before me as an empty canvas waiting to be painted with the colors of my soul!

chapter nineteen

Limbo

Bubbles, even magical bubbles, have a tendency to burst every now and then. One moment you are gently floating above life's worries and pain, and the next moment you find yourself being dropped into its muck and mire. Within in a few short weeks of reconnecting with Mother Earth, I felt as if my whole life had fallen apart.

My readings and income had dropped, and when I tried to use prayer, the law of attraction, and every other holistic ritual, idea, and trick that I had come across in the last twenty years, I had about as much success as I would have had by simply standing in my living room banging my head against the wall. It felt like I was walking through molasses; every step I took was agonizingly slow and seemed to drain me of energy without producing a single result.

By the end of December, I was in a panic about my finances and if it had not been for a Christmas gift from my father, I would have been unable to pay my bills for the first time since starting my business. I was frustrated, fearful, angry, and feeling abandoned by my own Spirit when I turned to Michael for an explanation.

"Little One, you are going through a period of limbo. You have been manifesting your life with the energy of fear for many years. Your

natural energy of Divine Love has a much higher vibratory frequency and is not compatible with your old energy. It is like changing the oil in your car; you must drain out all the old energy and flush the system of its sludge before you can replace it with a higher grade of oil. The time it takes to drain and flush the old energy and then fill you back up with the new energy is what we call limbo.

"During this time, you will experience physical, mental, and emotional exhaustion as you actually lose more energy from your physical being each day. You will need to pay special attention to your body and make sure that you exercise, eat well, sleep a full eight hours at night, and even take naps during the day whenever possible.

"You will not have enough energy to create anything new in your life, but prior to entering limbo, Spirit created all that you will need to get through this period. Once this process begins, there is nothing you can do to stop, hinder, or change the outcome in any way. You can only choose how to experience the process. Little One, you are a worrier, and if you choose to worry, you will experience a great deal of fear and discomfort in the next few weeks and months. But if you choose to relax and let go of your need to control the process, you may actually enjoy this time."

True to my nature, I chose to fight this process, and for the next month, I lived in a total state of panic and frustration. However, all my efforts to control the fear and sense of growing emptiness inside of me only resulted in a greater loss of control. I found myself buying things with my credit cards that I neither loved nor needed, and by the end of January, the life I had known was slipping away from me, and I was desperately holding onto it with only the tips of my fingernails.

Then just as I thought I was about to lose my mind, something strange happened. I woke up one morning and didn't feel scared or even worried. In fact, I didn't seem to have a care in the world. I felt joyous as I took Buddy for a walk, ate breakfast, and started the laundry. At lunch, I realized my mortgage payment was due at the end of the week, and while I didn't have the money at the moment, I somehow knew that everything would be taken care of. I realized that even though my credit card debt had increased over the last two months, my bills had always been paid on time, I had enough to eat, and no one I loved had disappeared from my life.

For the next few days, I even tried, unsuccessfully, to worry and experience fear. Finally I admitted to Michael, "I don't worry about things anymore."

"You have surrendered to your new Divine Purpose, Little One, but you still seem to be a little worried about not worrying."

It would take me a few more years to completely let go and trust Spirit to take care of me, but this first step made my life much easier. Looking back, I now see how much time and energy I invested in worrying about things that I had absolutely no control over. However, I needed to move through the intensity of these experiences to finally understand how humorous and overrated control and free will can be. Gaining that wisdom made it time well spent.

Once I moved through the limbo period, my energy greatly increased. I felt stronger, happier, more alert and aware of my surroundings. It was as if a light had turned on inside of me, lighting my path in the world. Then the magic began!

I started meeting new people and being offered gifts and opportunities that I had not asked for or even known that I wanted until they appeared before me. My holistic background had helped me attract what I had wanted in the past, but this was a step beyond the physical manifestation of my life on Earth. My prior creations had focused on the things I wanted, valued, and attracted from the physical world around me. These new gifts and opportunities were firmly anchored in what I had to offer the world, and gave me the total freedom to create everything I needed from within myself.

I no longer had to compromise or settle for the visions and creations of others; every gift was custom fit to my needs, desires, and vibratory frequency. The struggle to make things happen simply disappeared as I relaxed into the flow of Spirit and gently accepted each new gift and experience placed before me. It was wonderful, and I was confident that I had stepped into the new world of love and was about to experience nothing but peace, happiness, joy, and total enlightenment for the rest of my life on Earth!

This feeling lasted for about two weeks before my mind decided to challenge Spirit in an attempt to return to its previous position of power. I may have learned how to turn my mind off for short periods of time, but it was not about to throw in the towel and release its control over life in the physical world. After all, the human mind is of this world and seems to believe that Spirit has its own realm to play in. However, as my mind began to assert itself strange things began to happen.

My mind scheduled readings that were later cancelled, created experiences that were uncomfortable, bought material goods that I no longer wanted, and even attracted people that I did not like. Spirit on the other hand continued to bring unexpected magic and joy into my days. I felt like I was bouncing back and forth between the creations of what my mind wanted and what Spirit knew was best for me. I was not afraid or worried, but emotionally I wanted my mind and Spirit to get along, and it was clear that was not going to happen any time soon. This paradigm shift was turning out to be rather complicated, so I asked Michael for help.

"Little One, for millions of years, the human mind has been combining thoughts, emotions, and actions to create and experience the physical plane. In fact, the human mind was created to do just that. The vibratory frequency of Spirit cannot create fear, so the human mind volunteered to take on the task and has been doing so since the beginning of mankind's journey on Earth. The first Divine Purpose on Earth was to explore fear so this process of creating and experiencing fear was the most loving thing the mind could do.

"Without the consciousness of the human mind, this planet's paradigm shift would not be possible. Spirit unconditionally loves

the human mind and will not intrude into its processes. As long as the human mind chooses to take center stage in the manifestation of the planet, Spirit will step back, silently observe, and support its actions. The decision to shift into the new paradigm must be made within each individual human mind.

"Your human mind wants to make the shift into its new Divine Purpose, but does not know how to accomplish the task. We can help you with that process. The first thing you must do is fully embrace the mind and all that it has given you, not just in this lifetime but in all lifetimes. You must embrace your human mind as a creator of fear!"

I immediately tried to pull away from Michael and hide. I was so overwhelmed with shame, guilt, and embarrassment at what I saw in life after life on Earth that I started to sob uncontrollably. In each lifetime, I had successfully convinced myself that I was a good person that loved others and the planet, but in this moment, I felt only my complete and total love of fear.

I was faced with the reality that I loved anger, rage, lying, abusing and being abused, and controlling and manipulating people by asserting my ideas and will upon them. I had experienced lives of total fascination with death, war, and my own ability to destroy anything in the physical world that angered or irritated me. I had loved playing the martyr and dying for a cause, massing material wealth and power through greed and corruption, and separating myself so much from other humans and the life consciousness of the natural world that my actions seemed above reproach and beyond all physical consequences.

Then suddenly, I felt the rush of adrenaline coursing through my body as I pushed myself to the limits of survival in each of these lives. Fear had at times made me feel powerless, but more to the point, commanding fear had made me feel powerful in a way that I have never experienced in the Angelic Realm. This craving for adrenaline was unmistakable; I was addicted to fear!

"Little One, your entire planet is addicted to fear. You must step back and look at the wider picture. You fell in love with fear because you are the essence of love and loving fear is all you can do. You must fully embrace the gifts of fear and the pleasure that you have derived from its experiences in order to make the choice to move on to the next step in Earth's Divine Plan. The wisdom that you have gained is not about the nature of love and fear, it is about the expression of love and fear. In a world of duality, you cannot express one without the other. Surrender your shame, guilt, and embarrassment to us, and you will be free to take your first steps toward manifesting with Spirit."

I turned to face Michael and silently offered to surrender my addiction to him. Immediately, I began to relax as I felt all the negative thoughts and emotions of lifetimes of fear being stripped from my physical being. While I knew this process would take time, I already felt an overwhelming gratitude, understanding, and wisdom for the place that fear would now fill within my being. I still needed fear and its adrenaline rushes to keep my physical body safe on Earth, but its complete control over my physical being, mental focus, and emotions was already beginning to lessen. "I am ready Michael, what is my next step?"

"Honor your mind!"

chapter twenty

Honor Your Mind

"Little One, every belief system on Earth is incorrect, and every belief system on Earth is absolutely necessary for the oneness of Earth to exist!"

"Michael, do you realize that statement totally undermines my need to be right, not to mention 99% of the wars ever fought on this planet?"

"Yes." I had no idea where this conversation was going. *"Your next step involves the reformatting of your physical brain and its mental energy. Every belief system you have has been designed to allow you to create and experience fear, which was necessary in the old paradigm, but no longer serves you. We need to reset your mind to receive the higher energy frequencies that will allow you to focus on, perceive, and experience pure Divine Love from within your own physical body and the outer world."*

"Will this require surgery?"

"No, your Spiritual DNA has already started the process, but a few sessions of Jin Shin with Marsha Sterling will make the shift more comfortable."

Over the next few weeks, I had several sessions with Marsha and slowly began to feel a calming of my thoughts that I can only describe as meditating in full consciousness. My mind actually seemed to be releasing all those racing thoughts that had previously distracted me from the joys and pleasures of daily life. It was as if the silent observer within me was suddenly taking center stage in my mind. My consciousness also seemed to be manifesting more experiences and physical things in my life with less energy; my silent observer appeared to be very efficient!

"It's time to honor your mind, Little One. The human mind was given the daunting task of creating a world of fear, but it was also designed and made responsible for experiencing the world through its senses, assimilating the information received into new thoughts and belief systems, and then creating the next moment based on the totality of its experience. In the old paradigm your mind was constantly creating the world by pushing thoughts and feelings outward, and then pulling the experiences they created back towards it for its senses to experience.

"The human mind was constantly creating/experiencing/creating/ experiencing the slower vibratory frequencies of fear. The only time the mind could connect with the higher vibratory frequency of the Spirit was in the tiny space or gap between creating and experiencing. Over millions of years, humans began to focus more and more on the experiences they were creating in the outer world and less on the love of the Spirit within them, until they literally forgot their true essence.

"It is very difficult to give up something that you are good at, even when you know it is the right thing to do. Creating fear has become an addiction, and your brain will love and protect you no matter how hard you struggle to break free! You cannot create a new world of love by turning off, silencing, or controlling your mind, Little One, you can only create a new world by loving your mind. What do you want most for your mind? What is the most loving thing you can give your mind?"

"Peace of mind. I want my mind to let go of fear and be free to live in peace!"

"Then make it an offer."

Michael instructed me to sit down in a quiet place and take three deep breaths. I immediately felt Pink Lady come forward and enter the dark stillness of my human consciousness. She gently called out, *"Mind, show yourself,"* and then patiently waited for it to emerge.

Slowly, a beautiful soft yellow ball of light appeared in the darkness. As it moved towards Pink Lady, its surface began to change, and small flowery sprays that looked like yellow baby breaths began to pop up all over its surface. As the light within each individual spray began to pulsate, I could feel the symphony of my memories and life experiences contained within, and there was something else: curiosity!

Pink Lady then began the conversation with an introduction. *"We are the Spirit within, and we want you to know how much we love you and how important you are to us. We are aware that all of the changes that are occurring may lead you to believe that we are trying to get rid of you, no longer want or need you, and that we are ignoring all that you have to offer. We know that our renewed presence in your life threatens the survival of all that you have created. We assure you that we love everything about you and need you now more than ever. We honor all that you have done. You have created a wonderful world in which to explore and learn the nuances and details of fear and that is something we of Spirit could never have accomplished without you. You have great courage and physical stamina and have done all that has been asked of you and more. In fact, Viki loves you so much that she wants to give you a very special gift.*

"We are aware of how hard you have struggled to keep her safe and protected in a world of fear. We have silently watched as you have searched the outer world for the information and physical manifestations that will provide for all her needs. We have felt your exhaustion and frustration as you have sought to both create and

experience the world around you, all the while seeking answers to questions your world does not seem to understand. Mind, you have brought us to this moment of change and we ask you to join us in transformation.

"We offer you unconditional love through the energy of peace. We invite you to assume your true purpose of the expansion of love into the physical realm. Mind, you are a creation of Divine Love and you have earned the right to experience that love. You have raised the consciousness of humanity to a vibratory frequency that allows your eternal Spirit to enter your human body and begin the physical manifestation of love. You now have the opportunity to experience the peace that you truly are.

"We ask that you surrender the struggle of manifesting fear and allow yourself the luxury of simply experiencing all the love that Spirit has to offer. As you release the act of creating fear, you will find that you have additional energy with which to explore and enjoy your human experience. You will become more aware of everything in your physical world and you will have the time and energy needed to connect and communicate in peace with all life consciousness on the Earth plane.

"In addition, your spiritual DNA will begin to overlap your physical and spiritual senses allowing you to easily experience and assimilate inter-dimensional information into your daily life. You will not only see the world through your physical eyes, you will perceive all the colorful spiritual energy that flows through it. You will hear the voices of Angels, Fairies, and those of other realms as easily as those of humans. Your life will take on new depth and intensity as you touch, taste, and smell the sweetness of your physical planet and spiritual home in each moment.

"We know that you are very curious and love to explore and learn new things, so we have one more thing to offer: UNIVERSAL KNOWLEDGE!"

Pink Lady then reached out to my human mind and guided

it down into my Ascending Heart Chakra. My mind was looking outward from my body, and Pink Lady gently asked it to turn around, look inward, and find the doorway to universal knowledge. My mind immediately walked over, opened the door, and started to step in.

"Mind, you cannot enter this realm, for you are of the physical world, but you may ask any question at any time and simply reach in and pull out the answer. You will no longer have to expend huge amounts of energy searching, fighting, and compromising your beliefs to attain the information you desire; it will simply appear in front of you. Everything that is, was, or will be lies within the universal knowledge of the Angelic Realm and is yours for the asking."

As I silently observed my mind's first interactions with the energy of universal knowledge, I began to feel heat in my ascending heart chakra, a heat which soon began to move up the back of my neck and expand into my entire head. I felt a little dizzy and halfway expected to take off flying because this feeling was so similar to that of my entrances into the Angelic Realm. The connection lasted a few more minutes, and then a wave of pure peace ran through my entire body, and I knew that my mind had surrendered to its rightful place in my new Divine Purpose.

As my consciousness moved back into my head, I noticed something else in the shadows of my mind. It seemed to be hiding, yet I could feel its desire to come out into the open. Then I realized it was a memory from my infancy, and as I leaned into it, I felt the warmth of its truth. This was the memory of how I came to Earth with my Spirit and human consciousness joined in oneness, and I knew that the question my mind had asked at the doorway was, "Why did this split have to happen?" In that moment, I was not consciously aware of all the details my mind had received, but the peace I felt told me that my mind now understood that its journey had been both necessary and honored by Spirit.

Over the next few days, Michael explained to me that this was only the first baby step in the joining of mind and Spirit. *"Little One, you will find yourself bouncing back and forth between creating with the mind and creating with Spirit for the rest of this lifetime as you shift your addiction of fear to an addiction of love. Be gentle with yourself and do not judge or limit yourself when you find yourself creating fear in your life. Simply experience it with gratitude and move on. In time, your Spirit will actually teach the human mind how to create love, but that will take another hundred years or so."*

I was beginning to understand how I could change my individual manifestations on Earth, but I was curious about how the life consciousness of Earth was going to create an outer world of love. *"Little One, the creation of your new world takes place on an individual level. As you begin to align with Spirit, you allow its higher vibratory frequency to flow through your being and create the outer world.*

"The physicality of your world requires balance, so as higher energy flows in, lower energy dissolves. As of the winter solstice of 2007, approximately twenty percent of life consciousness was at least partially creating with the higher energy of love. By the summer of 2008, thirty percent of the energy moving into the outer world will be love-based, and the energy of fear will be rapidly diminishing.

"At that point, things may become very interesting on your planet. There will not be enough fear-based energy to support all of humanity's creations, and the foundations of many of your institutions that have been created or used to control, manipulate, abuse, or limit others will begin to crumble as love creates what is best for the oneness of the planet. Do not let fear confuse you; you no longer need fear to survive and all that you have created in love will continue to support you."

During Michael's explanation, I kept getting a strange visualization. When I was a child, I loved strawberry pop. The flavor was almost too sweet even for me, but I loved shaking the bottle and creating a beautiful pinkish fizz that dissolved on the tip of my tongue with the most refreshing burst of flavor imaginable.

Michael was amused and explained, *"When fear and love touch, the higher vibratory frequency of love begins to dissolve the lower energy of fear. This helps maintain the balance of the physical plane. As two life consciousnesses of Earth reach out to each other in love, any fear that lies between them will turn to fizz and begin to dissolve. As more and more life consciousnesses express love, every inch of your planet will be touched and filled with the sweetness of love."*

By the end of March 2008, I was beginning to see this pink fizz around people during readings, and it had become apparent that I was now seeing the world through rose-colored glasses!

chapter twenty-one

Like-Hearted

I have always loved the spring and its miracle of rebirth! I grew up in Illinois where grey winter skies often dragged on for months. Ever so slowly, the sun began to warm the air, and the grass turned green as the lilacs, tulips, irises, and other spring flowers suddenly burst into bloom. The world awakened in a vast array of color and life, and as a child I experienced an inner renewal of my physical being as well.

My birthday is April 11th and often coincided with the Easter season, which made it more special. I loved dressing up for Easter Church Services in my pastel dress and shoes and receiving a special Easter Basket filled with stuffed toys and all kinds of Easter eggs, marshmallow peeps, and chocolate bunnies! Throughout the years, I have continued to gift myself with an Easter outfit and basket, and the spring of 2008 was no different except for one thing.

My favorite Easter colors are sky blue, pale pink, and mint green, but this year I kept gravitating to bright yellow. Yellow is not a good color for me; wearing it brings out the blue undertones of my skin, making me appear a sickly green. Surrounding myself in yellow stimulates my desire to eat everything in sight. Still, everywhere I went, every outfit I tried on, and every bit of candy I bought reflected the color of yellow back to me. After a few weeks, I decided to investigate the possible spiritual implications of the yellow conspiracy that was invading my life.

I went into my sacred place and was immediately greeted by Pink Lady and Green Guy. Blue was on the mountaintop, Orange and Buddy were playing across the valley, and Purple was nowhere to be seen. Pink Lady told me they had someone for me to meet and led me to an open valley covered in yellow daffodils.

I felt her before I saw her. The softness of her energy swept over me, and I relaxed into a state of total peace. I closed my eyes and turned towards her, and even with my eyes closed, I saw her light so clearly that it fully penetrated my mind, body, and emotions. Her bright yellow skin was illuminated from within and accentuated her deep blue eyes. She was wearing a yellow headdress and long full gown, and appeared to float effortlessly above the daffodils. Only as I opened my eyes did she speak.

"Little One, I am Yellow and I ask to express the light of God through your physical body. My purpose is to bring Divine Truth into your life and allow you to express it through your words and actions. All that we create together will be of your higher purpose.

"The light of my female essence will join with that of Pink and Purple to create balance with your male essences of Blue, Green, and Orange, making it easier to share all of the gifts brought to you through the colors of your soul. Together we will link with humanity and the natural world of your planet, and my essence will allow you to connect directly with the souls of all organic life: rocks, minerals, water, air, electricity, and all other elements of your planet.

"My presence will allow you to BE one with your physical world and receive the information that will help the Angelic Movement to occur with ease and softness. Together we will help others to discover the Spirit within them and accept the Divine as commonplace in their lives.

"I am the expression of your eternal self and allow you to connect with Earth incarnations of both your past and future. I allow you to walk the Earth with a softness and vulnerability that creates the safety of love in each moment. I join with the heart of Pink, the healing of Green, the manifestation of Orange, the infinity of Blue, and Purple's intimate connection with Earth in perfect oneness and fulfillment. I am gentleness and truth, the end of your pain and the beginning of your humanity as it is meant to be expressed.

"I bring you the courage to accept, embrace, and express your true identity, and instill within you an irresistible desire to share your knowledge of the Angelic Realm with all those around you. Together we will walk out of the shadows of your false identity and into the light of a new day."

I could not speak; I could only feel Yellow's energy beginning to flow through my physical being. As I leaned into her, she wrapped me in her energy, and I fell into a deep peaceful sleep. Several hours later, I awoke with a sense of hope that I had not experienced since giving up my childhood dreams of riding my golden Unicorn through the enchanted forests and flying above the clouds on my black Pegasus.

Pal (Unicorn) and Happy (Pegasus) had been my source of power and strength during the first four years of my life. Sadly, when I gave up all hope of ever convincing my family and friends of the existence of my horses, their magic slowly disappeared from my view. I fell from the sky and found myself riding in the back seat of cars driven by adults, my freedom and power gone. The world had finally indoctrinated me into the belief that my magic was unacceptable, so I placed it in a tiny silver box, wrapped it with a pretty pink bow, and placed it deep within my heart where it would be protected and safe from anyone who wanted to take it away from me.

Over time, I forgot all about that magical box inside of me and created a new more practical human identity. I even found a sense of freedom driving my own car and convinced myself that I was a valued part of society because of all the things I had done and all the recognition my accomplishments had received.

Yellow had just reached into my heart, pulled out the silver box, and handed it to me. *"Little One, you are not important because of what you do, everything you do is important because of who you are."* I opened the box and, one by one, began to remember the magical gifts that I had brought to this planet. *"It is time to share yourself with others, Little One."*

I could feel my throat begin to constrict with fear and realized that I was still afraid of being rejected for my beliefs and being condemned for expressing my magic. My overwhelming need to protect my own unique gifts and relationship with Michael had forced me to present myself to the world as simply a channel. Michael and Yellow wanted more from me; they were asking me to bring all the love that I am to the world by accepting my worthiness as an equal partner to Spirit. Michael's words echoed in my mind, *"You must love yourself as you love me."*

Somehow, Yellow's presence ignited a new desire in me to express my magic. I was still afraid, but I felt driven from within to begin reaching out to the world in a new way. The addition of Yellow's energy made it easy and natural for me to BE me, and to do things that had previously made me very uncomfortable. Pink Lady was still my dominant personality, but Yellow was quickly expanding my true self into the world around me.

Within two weeks, I had created a format for opening a temporary Angelic Doorway that allowed groups of people to plug into and experience its energy for a few hours at a time. Michael and I then combined this experience with two-hour classes on a variety of Angelic topics. I had taught classes at a Community College in the past and hated it, mainly because I was expected to test my students and grade them accordingly, which felt both controlling and judgmental.

However, to my great surprise, my first few classes were very well attended, and I felt a great deal of love and warmth flowing from all of its participants. People really seemed interested in my relationship with Michael and the information we were providing, and I was fascinated by Michael's interactions with the group.

On one occasion, we were presenting information on how Angels connect with humans through the sense of smell when someone stood up in class and said they smelled an electrical fire. No one else smelled anything burning, but suddenly everyone began smelling something different. One individual smelled cookies baking, another person smelled roses, and others smelled lilacs, soap, spring rain, perfume, new leather, bread, and all sorts of other foods. There were other times when Michael would do mini-readings to get someone's attention, or suddenly conduct a guided meditation to make his point.

As I dutifully created my class outlines and then threw them away ten minutes into the class, another interesting thing began to happen. Once the matrix was opened, I could see strands of different colors connecting the people in front of me to the Angelic Realm. Many of these individuals had two or more colored strands, and I began to realize that multiple soul essences are very common. I don't know if we have always pulled multiple parts of our greater essence into the physical plane, but I know that at the present time on Earth, all of humanity is continuously expanding itself.

As I looked at the colors of other people's souls, I finally understood that no one was trying to take my magic away from me; everyone was just trying to find their own. My magic was lost when I chose to ignore Spirit and focus entirely on the information of the outer world. Magic was never meant to be hidden away for its own protection, it was always meant to be expanded into our world. The more love and magic we share, the more we receive.

I also discovered that my students asked questions that I would never have thought of asking. The information that Michael shared in the classes went far beyond our conversations and readings and at times conveyed very specific information about quantum physics, energy waves, and planetary changes. The world was becoming much more exciting to me, which further increased my desire to reach out and take part in the changes that humanity was facing. My introverted days appeared to be a thing of the past!

As my desire to share became instinctual within me, the feeling of belonging to a tribe in Wales returned, and I found myself longing to leave my relative isolation and connect with family. Since I lived thousands of miles away from my biological family, I knew I was looking for my Spiritual family or soul group.

I stated my intent to connect with Like-Minded people and set out to find my soul group. I attended a number of holistic classes, networking groups, churches, crafting groups, concerts, swim classes, animal rights groups, and on and on for several months. Strangely enough, I did not find one single group of people that I felt a true connection with. Just as I was about to give up and accept myself as an antisocial introvert, Michael said to me, *"Little One, you are asking for the wrong thing. You are not looking for Like-Minded people; you are looking for Like-Hearted people!"*

This statement hit me like a ton of bricks! I was not looking for people to share my beliefs with; I was looking for people to share my heart with. The instant that I began asking to surround myself with Like-Hearted People, my life began to change dramatically. I started connecting with everyone I met, and I felt loved and liked, playful and magical, and valued for simply who I am rather than for what I do.

The awe, wonder, and magic of my childhood was back in my daily life! As summer began, my heart was yearning to open a new doorway, and when I asked Michael if we could build a new matrix, he said, *"You already have, Little One."*

chapter twenty-two

Embracing Fear

Which came first, the chicken or the egg, the desire or the manifestation? I was feeling rather pleased with myself for creating a new matrix without even knowing it. I loved receiving a gift that I didn't ask for and didn't even know that I wanted.

For as long as I could remember, I had been afraid to ask for things because it always seemed that the one thing I asked for was the one thing that I never got. The gifts that I received were often very close to what I asked for, but somehow never seemed to fit perfectly, as if they were a quarter of an inch off.

When I asked Michael why that was, he said, *"You never really knew what you wanted, Little One. You have a way of letting other people tell you what you should have, should want, and should do. You put your trust in fear's amazing marketing machine!"*

"You're impressed with this marketing machine, aren't you, Michael?"

"It's one of the greatest feats of mankind. Humanity has used it for thousands of years to pull people into fear and keep them there. The old paradigm could never have been completed without it."

"So which came first, the chicken or the egg?"

"From an Angelic perspective, they are one."

Once I realized the new matrix had already formed within me, I felt like a kid in a candy store and wanted to discover every piece of it. What did it look like? What did it feel like? Where were we going to put it? When would we open it? What people would I meet along the way? What kind of intentions and ritual did I need? What gifts did I want to give and receive in the process?

My first meditation revealed a deep emerald green cylinder surrounded by a multitude of lush green colors. The waterfall was in an enclosed box canyon and appeared to be about the same height as the two previous falls. The cylinder's diameter was much larger than that of Melincourt and there seemed to be a large pool of water at its base.

While the vision of the waterfall was wonderful, it did very little to help me find its location, so I asked Michael and the universe for a little help. Within two weeks, I had turned on the television four times just as nature shows about Peru were airing, and had met six people who had just returned from or were going to Peru. I had dreamed of going to Machu Picchu for years and was getting very excited when Michael told me that while we were going to Peru, our destination was on the northeast side of the Andes. He said that the water from the falls would enter the Amazon River and flow across the continent to the Atlantic Ocean.

This information immediately caused a twinge of fear to ripple through my entire body. Jungles terrify me! I am uncomfortable in high heat and humidity, and I hate bugs, spiders, plants, and animals that sting and eat people. All the movies I had seen about the Amazon had giant anacondas and spiders the size of compact cars in them.

My protests seemed to have no effect on Michael, so I got on the computer and began looking for waterfalls in northern Peru. Unfortunately, I could find only descriptions and a few rather blurred pictures of the area. It took me about two more weeks to hone in on the department of San Martin and two waterfalls near the small town of Tarapota. One of the falls was listed as an hour walk into the jungle, but Ahuashiyacu Falls was described as approximately eighty feet tall with a pool at the bottom fit for swimming. It was also listed as a popular spot for tourists, so I assumed that not many people had been eaten by snakes while visiting there.

Michael assured me that Tarapota was our destination, and I began setting up the trip through a travel agency that offered hotel reservations and English-speaking tour guides. I also searched for Airline reservations to Lima through LAX, but every time I tried to make reservations, the plane was booked or the cost was too high.

When I asked Michael what was happening, he said, *"Free will is running rampant in that part of Peru right now. We can't take you into that area unless we know we can safely get you out. Go ahead and get your vaccinations, but hold off on the tickets and final confirmations for now."*

This is not a statement one wants to hear from an Angel. It appeared that not only did I have to contend with my fears of snakes and spiders, but malaria, yellow fever, civil protests, and rebel armies as well. Throw in a few piranhas, sharks, and flesh-eating bacteria and you have all of my greatest fears rolled up into one trip. Perhaps because of all these fears coming up in my face, the emotional preparation for this matrix turned out to be extremely difficult.

I started having recurring visions and nightmares of a male shaman and other tribal members performing dark magic in the area of the falls. I intuitively knew that these visions were of a past life in which I was a female who this man killed, but the details were blurred by my intense fear. Some of the fear I was feeling still existed in my relationships with males in my current life, and I knew it was time to heal those wounds.

My ritual and gifts for the opening of the Peru doorway would include clearing my mental, emotional, and physical body of my fear of male energy and opening my heart to the Divine God energy of Earth. It was a massive undertaking of stripping beliefs and emotions and building the physical strength of my body right up to the moment I left on the trip. However, by the end of June, I had completed my intentions and created the ritual. I still hadn't received the okay from Michael to buy plane tickets, but the flow of my energy in the Angelic Realm was moving in that direction.

Soon after completing my ritual, some rather unusual activity began to occur in my mediations and dreams that seemed totally unconnected with the Peru doorway. Michael had always told me that multitasking is overrated, so when I began hearing clicking noises in my head and swimming with dolphins in my dreams, I was both intrigued and confused. There are no dolphins in the mountains of the Andes! After about a week, I asked Michael what the Angels were doing and he simply said, *"It's not us."*

"Who is it?"

"It's the dolphins on your planet."

"What do the dolphins want?"

"They would like you to open a matrix in the ocean."

"Why?"

"Ask them." Sometimes talking to Michael is like pulling teeth!

I went into meditation and found myself in an underwater world surrounded by six large dolphins. The dolphins took me to a reef and asked me to put a matrix at the site. They explained that they needed the energy of the Angelic Realm to heal and protect their physical bodies from the toxins being created by the drilling in the Gulf of Mexico. The sediment that is being brought up from below the ocean floor contains cadmium and other heavy metals that are harmful to both their babies and their adult reproductive systems. The dolphins hoped to use the pure Angelic energy to heal the damage within them, and to create a safety zone for their species. I told them I would do whatever I could to help them.

The moment I came out of meditation, Michael said, *"The doorway will need to be opened in the ocean floor and the energy pulled upwards. The matrix will be anchored approximately fifty*

*feet below the surface in a small canyon-like area which will help
to create an intense area of energy that the dolphins can use in a
variety of ways."*

I could almost see the blue energy flowing out from the bottom
of the ocean as Michael spoke, and I knew the matrix was already
forming within my physical body. It was a joyous feeling suddenly
interrupted by the words *"fifty feet below the surface."*

*"Little One, you need to learn how to scuba dive and get certified
within the next two months."*

I had always been intrigued by scuba diving, but three huge
problems had railroaded my attempts in the past. I have no core body
strength and a weak left knee, which prevents me from carrying
the tanks on my back outside of the water. I am extremely buoyant
and have difficulty staying underwater. Lastly, scuba diving is very
expensive.

Nevertheless, I called a local diving center and told them that in
spite of all my difficulties, I would like to learn to scuba dive. I was
informed that they were running a special price on certification, but
I would have to start classes the next day in order to be certified in
time for my trip. The instructor I spoke with was confident that he
could teach me how to put the tanks on in the water and use weights
to control my buoyancy.

I accepted the challenge and was certified at Blue Hole, New
Mexico in August. Even with the weights, I had difficulty controlling
my ascents and was terrified of attempting an ocean dive. Michael
suggested that I open up the doorway during a PADI Buoyancy
Certification dive in order to deal with the problem. This would place
an experienced instructor with me during the dive for added safety.
This reassured me, and I went back into meditation with the dolphins
to discover the location of the dive.

The dolphins took me back to the same reef, and I patiently
explained to them that I was human and needed something above
the water to find the site, so they took me to the surface and showed

me a boat in the distance. Interspecies communication is fun even when unproductive! I asked the Angels for help and immediately began tasting something extremely sweet with a thick texture and recognized it as molasses. I then googled Molasses Reef and saw an underwater picture of the site the dolphins had been showing me. The matrix was to be placed off the coast of Key Largo, Florida, near the home of the dolphins that had touched my heart twelve years earlier.

Two days later, Michael said we could safely get in and out of Peru, but it would be a quick trip. We would then go to Key Largo and open the second matrix. Within forty-eight hours, I was able to get plane tickets through Miami International Airport, confirm hotel reservations and an English-speaking tour guide, set up a dive on Molasses Reef with a PADI instructor, and inform my dad that I would be visiting for a few days in October. I still felt great apprehension about every detail of the trip, but Michael continued to assure me it was safe, and my desire to open the matrixes overwhelmed any sense of fear that I had.

"Little One, you will return home with very little fear left within you!"

chapter twenty-three

Cataratas Falls

As a child, my greatest fear was physical pain. I spent the first thirteen years of my life waiting for the dull ache that wrapped around the right side of my torso to explode into sharp stabbing pains that paralyzed my whole body. I tried to figure out how to stop the pain by limiting my physical activity, watching what I ate, wearing loose fitting clothes, and going to the bathroom every hour. But nothing worked until a surgeon corrected the problem. Unfortunately, by that time, the fear of my own body had become firmly entrenched in every aspect of my life.

In the summer of 2008, I finally realized that much of my need to deny and distance myself from Earthly experiences stemmed from those early fears and that I would never be able to fully experience the joy of being in a physical body until I faced them. The night before I left on my trip, I was still feeling apprehensive, so Michael suggested that I set as my intention for the trip, Spirit will never ask anything of me that I cannot do. I ended my nightly meditation with this statement and fell asleep wrapped in Michael's energy.

I awoke the next morning feeling safe, secure, and excited about my new adventure. My magical bubble was back! The next twenty-four hours were a whirlwind of travel from Colorado Springs to Dallas to Miami and then a night flight to Lima that arrived at 4:30 the next morning. My trip was fun—all my flights were on time, there was plenty of time to relax and eat during my layovers, I met several wonderful traveling companions along the way, and my arrival in Lima was very interesting. There were several aggressive men who approached me in the airport offering to assist me with luggage and buy me drinks, but I was in the presence of Michael, and a quick no thank you diverted their attention to others.

In the past, their behavior would have made me very uncomfortable, but on this occasion I just found it amusing, although that may have had more to do with my jet lag than the situation. Luckily, Lima Airport makes all its announcements in both Spanish and English, so navigating my way around was easy.

After purchasing a crystal for my ritual, I boarded my plane to Tarapota, relaxed into my seat, and fell asleep. Sometime later, Michael woke me up and asked me to look out the window at the clouds below. Suddenly, we reached the edge of the cloudbank and the Andes rose up to greet me. They were magnificent and so close that I felt like I could reach out and touch them.

The energy of these mountains was unlike anything I had ever felt before and yet somehow familiar. There was an incredible softness accompanied by a powerful feeling of isolation. I felt almost no sense of human energy emanating from this place, yet the power of Mother Earth reached out to invite me into her gentle soul. Years before, I had been taught in my shamanic studies that South America holds the Heart Chakra of the Earth, and in this moment, I gratefully experienced that energy.

I was mesmerized by every peak and valley, and I wondered about the people living in the tiny villages below me, separated from each other and the outside world by miles and miles of rugged roads and paths. What must it be like to exist in a world of such Earthly magic? I was looking at extreme physical isolation, all the while knowing that no aloneness could exist here. The purity of Mother Earth was just too strong.

Then I saw the Amazon in all its glory. It was a huge glistening brown and gold ribbon cutting through the jungle. I could not see its beginning or end, and it reminded me of the infinity that I felt in the Angelic Realm the first time I expanded into the colors of my soul. Unlike the isolation of the Andes, this body of water seemed to link all life together. Just the thought of Angelic energy flowing within it expanded me, and in that moment I knew that nothing could stop me from opening this new doorway.

As we landed in Tarapota, the energy created by humans quickly took over. I felt a wave of shock at the poverty that surrounded me. The airport was one of the few concrete buildings, and while the town was in the process of completing its first water treatment plant, most of the people lived in metal huts without running water. There were people picketing at the airport, but since I couldn't read or speak Spanish, I had no idea why.

I was met by my tour guide, Lenin, who was a very cute nineteen-year-old male who spoke perfect English. Lenin would be the only person that I would be able to verbally communicate with during my stay. I immediately connected with him and was soon amazed to learn that he had completed his schooling (like all children in Tarapota) at the age of fifteen. He then taught himself English from a Spanish/English dictionary in order to work with tourists and make money.

Lenin had decided he would learn one hundred words in English each week and used the pronunciation guide in the dictionary to learn how to say the words and put sentences together. I have tried to learn Spanish on numerous occasions and have been able to learn only a handful of phrases, so this accomplishment just boggled my mind. Lenin's desire and dedication to learning were inspiring! He also had a cell phone, which seemed to be permanently attached to his ear; I guess teenagers around the world aren't so different after all.

We were taken to the Hotel in a van, which I soon discovered was a luxury reserved for tourists. Most people travel by bicycle and motorcycle. Lenin and I shared dinner and made plans for my tour to the waterfall the next morning. I explained to him that I would be doing a meditation and spiritual ritual at the falls. When I told him I talked to Angels, he seemed both amused and accepting.

After he left, I took a walk around the hotel's gardens, lagoon, and other grounds. The facility was full, and since I could not communicate with anyone, I found myself in a position of silent observer. I was amazed by how much I learned about others simply by watching. As I went to bed that night, I reflected on how much energy and focus I usually place on what I want to say and do in my interactions with others and how that prevents me from seeing many of the gifts others have to share. Simply observing allowed me to BE in the experience without expectations of myself or others. It was both relaxing and refreshing, and I fell asleep feeling comfortable and safe.

On October 10, 2008, I awoke unusually energized and began to get dressed. Michael immediately told me that I was wearing the wrong thing and asked me to put on my bathing suit under my cutoffs and tee-shirt and wear my beach shoes. I changed and when Lenin arrived, he immediately told me that the road to the waterfall had been closed and we would not be able to get there.

I asked if it would be opened the next morning and he made a phone call and found out the road would be closed for at least a month. This did not feel like part of my magical bubble, and I wanted to know why Michael would bring me thousands of miles to a waterfall I could not get to! *"Little One, ask about the other waterfall."*

I asked Lenin if there was another waterfall in the area and he said yes, but it was a forty-minute motorcycle ride into the hills, then an hour walk into the jungle, and outsiders rarely go there. It was ninety-eight degrees and climbing, but I did not hesitate, I simply asked him to take me there and he agreed, with the understanding that I would pay for the gas. I still did not hesitate when the hotel and tour company required me to sign a four-page waiver written in Spanish before we left, or when we came to a road block in the hills thirty minutes later where we paid two men holding very large rifles to let us through. I was with Michael and I knew in my heart that I would be fine as long as I kept my hat on and said nothing!

It was well over a hundred degrees by the time we reached the trailhead, and twenty minutes later, I was getting a little concerned about my physical condition. My body was exhausted from the heat and I was not sure I could continue, but Lenin kept encouraging me. A few minutes later, he nonchalantly told me we needed to cross the river.

The water was just above my knees, very cold, and it totally reenergized my body. Once I was wet and cool, I felt like I could do anything! The hike then became fun and Lenin began to point out all the plants that his family harvested for food. We even tasted a few. At one point, we were greeted by Howler monkeys that threw twigs at us, but I saw no snakes or spiders. Lenin explained that there were no large snakes in this area, but offered to take me to Iquitos, which was an hour away and a thousand feet lower in elevation where we could see fifteen-foot snakes and spiders that were eight inches across. I politely declined; hoping my willingness to face my fears was enough to release them.

We continued on for almost forty-five minutes until we came to a very large hill with steps cut into its side. Each step was almost knee high and about half way up, I became dizzy. It became very painful to take a breath, and I could hardly lift my feet off the ground. I sat down and told Lenin I could go no further. Lenin stopped for a few minutes to let me catch my breath and then simply informed me that we were almost there and he knew I could do this. I silently asked Michael and my body if I could make it to the falls, heard a quiet yes, and found the strength to climb to the top of the hill.

Once we reached the top, we started to cross the river a second time. About halfway across, the water suddenly rose to our armpits and the current began to increase. Lenin stopped and asked me if I knew how to swim, and while I wanted to laugh out loud at this new turn of events, I knew he was concerned and just said, "Yes, I'm a good swimmer."

Needless to say, we made it across the river. Over the next hour, I stopped to catch my breath and begged to turn around three more times as Lenin assured me we were almost to the falls. Finally, I sat down and told Lenin in no uncertain terms that I could go no further. He just looked at me and said, "The falls are just around that bend." I wasn't sure I believed him, but I got up and walked to the bend anyway.

It was exactly as I had seen it in my visions, and it took my remaining breath away! The water fell from a cliff eighty feet above the surface of a pool that was almost twice the size of the matrix that we had placed in Wales. The pool reflected the shades and hues of the sky and jungle that completely surrounded it, and the cool water beckoned me to enter and begin my ritual.

Lenin knew I needed to be alone and disappeared up another trail that led to the top of the falls. I had written my ritual on index cards and placed them in my pocket along with the crystal that I needed to open the doorway. The words of the ritual had disappeared with our second river crossing, so I pulled out the crystal and simply opened my heart to this place, to the Angelic Realm, and to all of Mother Earth.

I walked into the water, released the matrix, and silently watched the cylinder form at the edge of the pool as the bordering trees and plants disappeared behind it. It was emerald green with just a few flecks of yellow and white dancing through it, and it filled the water around me with a soft luminescence. Michael then asked me to look up, and I saw the doorway open and a brilliant white light burst through the dark tint of my sunglasses. I swam closer and closer to the base of the waterfall, drawn towards it as a moth is drawn to the flame, mesmerized by its gentle softness.

"Little One, stand up."

I was in chest-high water when my feet found a soft level surface among the rocks to stand on. Immediately, I felt myself drawn into the Earth and surrounded by a lattice of living crystal. I melted into this structure and could feel myself encircle the entire planet.

Then it spoke to me, *"We are the crystalline structure of the Earth. We hold the consciousness and power that will fuel the creation of a new world of love. Over the next few years, we will activate all the colors of the Angelic Realm within us, and in time we will serve as the power source for the entire planet. Through us, Mother Earth will provide all the abundance that is needed to care for her children. Each life consciousness on Earth holds an individual crystalline structure within them, which, once activated, will connect them directly with Mother Earth and all the love she has to offer. We invite you to begin the activation of your crystalline structure now."*

I accepted the offer and was suddenly transported back to the pool and realized it had started sprinkling. As I looked towards the falls, I saw a blue ball hovering above the water near the base of the falls. I had never seen an orb before and assumed this must be what I was looking at. Then I heard Lenin calling out to me. He had seen a storm over the mountains from the top of the trail and said we needed to go. If it started raining the trail would become impassable and we would have to spend the night in the jungle.

My heart longed to stay here forever, but Michael was urging me out of the water, so after one more moment of gratitude, I returned to the bank and we started back. I had spent less than thirty minutes at Cataratas Falls and intuitively knew that while I would never return in this lifetime, a part of me would remain forever in this beautiful jungle.

The trip back was much easier; I was over-energized from the Angelic energy and I could still feel the crystalline structure beneath my feet. The trail and its agonizing steps were now downhill, and it took about a third of the time to return to the motorcycle as it had taken to get to the falls. It was late afternoon when we arrived back at the hotel. I took a shower and sat down on the bed feeling both stunned and overwhelmed by what had happened. "Michael, this was the waterfall of my visions. Why didn't you tell me I had the wrong site?"

"If I had, Little One, you would not have come. You would have let your fears and the belief that your body was not strong enough to make the hike into the jungle stop you. So often, humans allow the fears of their minds to dictate what their bodies can and will do. We had to put you into a situation where your heart's desire to express love exceeded the fears of your mind."

"How did I do it, Michael? My body has never had this type of endurance before."

"You were in a place of Divine Love and totally present in your body, and when it tested you and asked you to rest, you did. For the first time in your entire life, you trusted your body and it trusted you. Love and trust allow you to utilize all of your mental, emotional, and physical power, which makes all things possible. We also sent Lenin to help you. He could see within you what you could not see, the power of your love. No human ever walks the Earth without assistance.

"Little One, what do you feel?"

"I feel deep intense love for both myself and this doorway. It's as if the struggle to reach the falls makes this matrix even more special to me."

"Does it make you feel more worthy?"

"Yes."

"Why?"

"Because for the first time in my life, I gave everything that I am and my body didn't let me down."

"Are you in pain?"

"No, I don't seem to have a scrape or bruise anywhere on my body and I'm not sore. Why am I not sore?"

"Love never hurts, Little One."

The next morning, I ate breakfast and went for a final walk along the river near the hotel. I came across a woman sitting on the other side of the river, washing her clothes and gathering water in earthen pots. Nearby were two children—a toddler who was giggling and dripping water all over a smaller baby who was laughing joyously. I started laughing as I observed them, and then I noticed the mother watching me. As our eyes met, we smiled and shared the joy of her children. Being silent observers allowed the two of us to melt into the purest form of communication: oneness of the heart.

Two hours later, I was at the airport. Lenin made sure I was checked in and ready to go and then headed out to his next assignment. As he waved and jumped into the van, I suddenly felt a wave of recognition flow through my body; Lenin was the Shaman of my nightmares! Yet in the last two days, we had successfully turned control and manipulation into support and encouragement. Terror had been replaced with play and fear had been transformed into love. I had spent just forty-eight hours in Tarapota, but as I flew out of the town, I could no longer see its poverty; I could only see the love and magic of its people and the beauty of the jungle that surrounded them.

I flew out of Lima that night and was awakened somewhere east of Panama by a large lightning storm below us. I watched the lightning change color as it moved about the clouds and wondered if this is what the crystalline structure would look like as it began to awaken its new energy and Divine Purpose.

chapter twenty-four

Molasses Reef

Silent observation comes in many forms. I had just left a country where I could not speak the human language, and I was about to enter a world where no human language existed. There had been a few varieties of fish in Blue Hole springs, but this was my first entrance into an ecosystem that covers two-thirds of our world and is filled with life so diverse and colorful that it seems to bend the perceptions of the human mind to its will. Underwater, everything looks bigger and closer, sounds travel greater distances, and all life takes on a weightlessness and freedom unknown to landlocked humans.

It was precisely this weightlessness that concerned me. On my previous dives, my extreme buoyancy had left me unable to control my movements in the water. In a spring only sixty feet deep and a few hundred yards across, it's hard to get lost, but the open ocean is another story. How would I find the exact spot to open the matrix, and would I be able to stabilize my movements long enough to complete the task?

I arrived in Key Largo physically and mentally exhausted after only four hours of sleep on the plane and then a two-hour drive from the airport. However, I was emotionally energized and my bubble was still intact. The motel clerk said my room would be ready in an hour, so I ate breakfast, confirmed my dive for the next morning, and then checked in and slept for eight hours. I awoke refreshed and hungry, and after eating dinner, went back to the room to perform the ritual for the new matrix. After setting my intentions, I asked Michael if there was anything else I needed to do and he simply said, *"No matter what is in front of you, go with the flow."*

At breakfast the next morning, I was feeling strong and self-assured and could not help wondering why I was not experiencing any fear. These feelings continued as I arrived at the Dive Center, completed the video portion of my training, and picked up my rental equipment. As I tested my equipment, one of the fins seemed loose. When I asked to try on another one, I was told they didn't have any more. I found this strange since they rent diving equipment, and while having my needs ignored would have normally irritated me, Michael had said go with the flow so I did.

I was then introduced to my dive instructor, and we went back to the hotel and completed the pool portion of my certification. An hour later, just before getting on the boat, I used my crystal to open the matrix within me and then offered it to Michael for placement on the ocean floor.

We arrived at Molasses Reef to find three-foot waves. That doesn't sound nearly as large as it looks or as powerful as it feels. I was terrified of getting into the water and was having trouble moving on a rocking boat with a forty-pound tank strapped to my back and an additional eighteen pounds of weights in my vest and belt. The crew tried to throw out a line, but it was forced against the boat by the waves, and I had visions of being carried out to sea before I could even get under the water.

Then Michael said, *"Jump in the water, we are with you,"* and I jumped in the water. I let the air out of my vest and still could not get underwater until my dive instructor squeezed the air out of the shoulders of my vest and literally pushed me under. The first taste of salt water at the corners of my mouth was shocking, but the water entering my wet suit was warm and encouraging as I began to descend towards the reef below.

The current below the surface seemed almost as strong as the waves and after a moment of resistance, I heard Michael again say, *"Go with the flow,"* so I relaxed and let it take me. The visibility was extremely poor as the water took on a brown cast from the silt, sand, and small pieces of marine plants being thrown around in the current. I could not see my instructor, but I could feel Michael around me and I felt totally safe. I checked my watch and waited, and within a minute, my instructor and another diver found me and I began to follow them across the reef. The two of them were experienced divers and much stronger swimmers and I found myself lagging behind.

About fifteen minutes into the dive, the instructor led us down to the bottom of the reef and motioned to both of us to look under a low rocky ledge. I waited my turn and then discovered a huge brown eel curled up in the back corner. It had an enormous head and was larger than any snake I had ever seen. Its eyes seemed to glow as its body undulated in the current. I just wanted to get away from it and realized that perhaps the willingness to face my fears and actually facing them were two different things.

Then it happened! I lost my right fin. It just seemed to fall off. I was less than four feet away from a very large eel, experiencing negative buoyancy in a very strong current, trying to retrieve my fin, and watching my dive partners swim away. The fin was lying on the bottom of the reef and as I tried to force my right foot into it, my left foot also touched the ocean floor. (For all you divers out there; yes I know it is a cardinal sin to touch any part of the reef while diving!)

The moment that both of my feet touched the bottom, the matrix shot up through my body and out my crown chakra. Time suddenly stopped, the ocean stood still, and amidst total quiet, I saw the aqua blue cylinder begin to form around me. It was only then that I noticed that I was in the canyon that the dolphins had shown me in my dreams. As the energy in the cylinder moved upwards, it began to flow over the canyon perimeter, and like a flower opening to the sun, the blue energy filled the sea in an ever widening circle of blue light. I felt a burst of heat rush through my entire body and then flow out my heart chakra and slowly begin to merge with the clear blue energy surrounding me.

A sudden rush of noise and the force of the current began to pull me off the ocean floor, and I began to swim towards my dive partners. I paused for a moment to see the eel stick its head out of its cave and watched two separate schools of colorful fish riding the energy as it flowed out of the canyon. I wondered what the inhabitants of this underwater world would do with this energy.

There were at least eighteen other divers on the reef, but no other human noticed the miraculous event that had just occurred. I was forced to question what world I was really most in tune with. Was my identity as a human suddenly being altered by the magic of crystalline structures, the natural world of land and sea, and the great love being offered by Mother Earth? Would I ever be able to forgive myself for humanity's abuses and cruelty towards the natural world? I suddenly felt more afraid of humanity than anything that existed in the natural world.

We continued our dive and as my tank was approaching the half-full mark, I realized this was where my problem staying underwater usually occurred. I tried to signal my instructor, but he and the other diver were too far away to notice, so I asked Michael if there was anything left to do to complete the matrix. He quietly said, *"The dive will be complete when you see the shark."*

I thought he was kidding until I saw a shadow a few yards above me. At first, I just assumed it was another diver, but when I looked up, the shark was directly above me. It was slightly longer than me and dark blue in color. I was mesmerized as it effortlessly swam over me without the slightest acknowledgment of my presence. I stopped swimming and watched as it moved in and out of several small coral reefs and then disappeared into the ocean.

A few minutes later, I found myself being forced upward to the surface and although I struggled to stay under, found myself being tossed about in the waves. The waves were so high that I needed help from the crew to get back on the boat. When my instructor and the other diver returned about fifteen minutes later, I wondered if they had even missed me.

We were scheduled for a second dive on another reef and I had not completed the ocean part of my Peak Buoyancy Certification. I was tired and more than a little hesitant about getting back in the water and asked Michael what to do. *"Little One, we cannot keep you safe at the next site, stay on the boat."* I took off my gear and celebrated with chocolate! As I filled out my dive notes, I realized that the matrix had been opened at forty-seven feet, and was later informed by the other divers returning to the boat that the second reef had been filled with jellyfish, not something I would have wanted to uncontrollably ascend through!

I returned to the motel, showered, and went out to dinner. On the way back to my room, I stopped to watch the sun set and listen to the water gently caressing the dock just outside my room. My dreams were filled with the clicks, whistles, and songs of dolphins as they danced in an underwater world of aqua blue energy, and I awoke before dawn to the sound of rain and Michael telling me to get up. I protested, saying it was raining. *"Then put your bathing suit on, Little One."* I blindly obeyed and walked out the door of my room and down a dirt path to a small wooden pier where Michael suggested I sit down.

The rain had diminished to a few sprinkles and the first rays of sunlight were peeking through the clouds. I closed my eyes and was almost asleep when I heard a splash. I could immediately feel the dolphin's power. He was over six feet in length and had to be at least five hundred pounds. I stayed very still as he swam by the pier twice, and then I lay down and stretched my hand out into the water. He swam back and rubbed the entire length of his body across my hand.

I had touched captive dolphins before, but never a wild dolphin. Tears started flowing from my eyes. I felt honored and humbled by this creature's willingness to make a connection. As he swam away, I saw two more dolphins, a mother with a very small baby. I remained still with my hand in the water and the mother, keeping her body between her baby and me, came and ran her body across my hand. The two dolphins circled and the mother then placed the baby between her body and me, and gently guided her child to my hand. I watched the three of them until they disappeared into the open ocean, thanked Michael, and hoped we had done enough to save these beautiful creatures and all of their children.

chapter twenty-five

Let Me Be The One

"Little One, why do you think I am male?"

I had just returned from opening two doorways where I had asked to receive the gift of healing with males, so I was pretty sure this was a trick question. "Well, your name is Michael, and all of the pictures of you that I have seen throughout my life depict you as a male."

"That is why the world sees me as male. Why do YOU see me as male?"

"It's a lot of things. The first time I met you was at a channeled reading done by a man and it sounded very harsh to me. You said some things to me that hurt my feelings and scared me.

"Do only males hurt your feelings and scare you?"

"No, but the energy behind the words was so overwhelming that I felt physically threatened, and I usually don't feel that way in confrontations with other females."

"Little One, do you remember when you first felt physically threatened by men?"

"I think I have always been threatened by men."

"Your fear did indeed begin almost the moment you were born, Little One. You were held too long in the birth canal and the excess

fluid in your nasal cavities and lungs made it difficult for you to take your first breath. You were actually delivered between the parking lot and the front door of the hospital, where there were no medical supplies. The only thing available to the male doctor that delivered you was a tank of ether and he forced a shot of it into your lungs to make you shiver and take a breath.

"This act saved your life, but also destroyed your olfactory nerve, which is why you have no physical sense of smell. It also immediately created the belief system within you that in life and death situations you are powerless against the physical actions of males. This pattern of male doctors using force to save your life was repeated several times in your childhood. During the kidney surgery, another male doctor unknowingly damaged your right ovary, which reduced your body's ability to make estrogen and diminished your future sex drive."

As Michael revealed this information, I felt anger, rage, sadness, and an incredible sense of loss. As the tears began to flow, I also felt intense fear. I remembered sitting in the kidney specialist's office after enduring a very painful set of x-rays, listening to the doctor explain to my parents that I had a kidney defect that needed to be corrected. I could still hear the sound of his voice as he said, "We'll slit her open and fix the problem."

No one asked me if I wanted to be cut open or even seemed to notice that I was in a state of pure panic. I didn't know that I would be asleep for the surgery and thought that I would be able to feel the pain of being cut open and see all the blood and organs inside of me. I felt helpless, powerless, and I believed I was about to die.

"Little One, when someone inflicts trauma upon another, even with the best of intentions, fear is created. You have recreated the traumas of your birth and surgical invasions over and over in more forms and experiences than you can count in an attempt to release your fears and heal your body, mind, and emotions. Through this process, your mind validated all male energy as harsh and forceful

*and expanded your belief that females are powerless and helpless.
We do applaud your ability to control and manipulate men to get
what you want and keep you safe, but it is time for you to learn the
Divine Truth about male energy on your planet so you may embrace
and enjoy it.*

*"Male energy on the Earth plane is not harsh and forceful. FEAR
IS HARSH AND FORCEFUL! In the old paradigm, all relationships
on Earth promoted spiritual growth through mirroring, sharing,
and creating fear. Males on your planet are genetically made to be
physically stronger, and that creates a tendency for males to be more
physically forceful.*

*"However, the tendency for females is to be much more emotionally
forceful, which can cause as much pain as physical force. Little One,
you have confused emotional force with love; however, it is actually
just another form of fear. Many females mentally and emotionally
force males into being their protectors and providers. Taking on the
full responsibility of keeping the family safe and financially secure
can actually increase the fear in males, making them more controlling
and forceful.*

"Do I feel male to you when you are in the Angelic Realm?"

"No, in the Angelic Realm, I don't feel male and female energy. I
simply feel the essence of love melting in and out of oneness. I have
never thought about it before, but now that you ask, I must admit that
I can only tell you, Uriel, and the other Angels apart by melting into
pieces of wisdom and experience that we have shared outside of the
Angelic Realm."

*"So does my energy still feel harsh and overwhelming to you as
you sit on the Earth in this moment?"*

"No, it is the softest, most non-intrusive energy I have ever
known."

"Then why do you think I am male?"

It was a trick question. "Michael, I think of you as a male because
I want you to be male. I want you to take care of me and be my

protector. The power of your energy beside me helps me feel more powerful, balanced, and whole on the planet. In the midst of your consciousness, I am stronger, softer, and willing to love."

"Little One, you asked to receive the gift of healing with males on your planet, and the doorways have given you everything that you need. Lenin is one of the first males to step out of the old energy of fear and into the new energy of love. His very male energy supported, encouraged, and mirrored all the love in your heart back to you. In his presence, you became stronger, softer, and more powerful than you have ever been in this lifetime. You reached out to the world with a great gift and embraced all the power the crystalline structure had to offer. You had fun and experienced total and complete joy as you released all limitations of being in a female body.

"Your dive instructor on Molasses Reef still resides in the fear-based world. There was no support or encouragement, and your needs were dismissed and ignored before, during, and after the dive. Yet you completed your task with awe and wonder. You provided your own sense of safety, took care of yourself, and found the strength within you to open the doorway while loving everything around you, including a shark. Perhaps most importantly of all, Little One, you released your fears of harshness and chose to stop fighting with the males on your planet.

"Little One, there is another reason you think of me as male."

My consciousness was immediately transported to another place and time. I was a very large-winged humanoid female. My powerful copper-colored body was at least sixteen feet tall with an equal wingspan. I was dressed as a warrior and carried a heavy metal shield and sword. I immediately knew my world was fighting for its survival.

We had been invaded by the inhabitants of another planet who were obsessed with destroying our entire species. Thousands of people of all ages had gathered on the mountainside to prepare for what would most likely be our final battle; in this day, we would prevail or we would die. Then he landed on the peak above us—our leader, protector, military strategist, and last hope. We listened intently to his final instructions, inspired by his belief that our love for our planet and each other would lead us to victory.

He was my partner, the father of my children, and an individualized strand of the Angel I now know as Archangel Michael. We did prevail and our species and world did survive, but the cost was immense. We lost almost half of our parents, children, siblings, and friends. It would take hundreds of years and many generations to heal the physical destruction of our planet. Michael would return through incarnation after incarnation until the healing of this world was complete.

This was the first time that Michael had ever let me see an individualized strand of his consciousness and I was overwhelmed with gratitude. As an incarnate being, I suddenly understood why this Archangel had never incarnated on Earth. Michael holds the wisdom and knowledge of fear within his consciousness; he led a world through its darkest hour. This time, Michael has chosen to expand his spiritual essence by guiding his armies on Earth into love. Michael knows that the moment one enters the physical realm, fear is required and to lead us back to love he must remain the pure essence of love, melting into oneness with each and every life consciousness of Earth.

I also understood where all the pictures of Archangel Michael around the world and in different religions came from. There are perhaps millions of people currently on Earth that knew and loved Michael throughout his lifetimes on that far away planet. We remember him and long to feel the power that once protected us and now guides us back to the light of love. I believe that within us is more than just the memory of Michael. I believe we each carry a piece of his knowledge and strategy of how to move from fear to love, and because of this, our journey to love will prevail!

I knew the next step in my path was to embrace the pure God energy waiting to be expressed by the males of this planet. Only then would I be able to fully express Divine Love through my own Goddess energy and create loving relationships. However, there seemed to be very few people around me that were ready to let go of fear and begin expressing pure love, so I asked Michael, "Where do I begin?"

"Begin with me, Little One. Let me be the one! Let me be the Angel that heals you and walks the Earth beside you."

chapter twenty-six

My Pledge

In an instant, I experienced the thread of my life within the eternal tapestry of creation. Hearing Michael say "me" instead of "we" and allowing me to see an individualized strand of his consciousness, altered every perception, belief, and feeling that I had ever had in this lifetime. For a brief moment, I knew how the very fabric of consciousness wove itself into the infinite creation of love.

By following Michael's journey through both the Angelic Realm and the physical universe, I was able to trace mine—connecting one life to another, one purpose to another, even one realm to another— constantly expanding outward into new experiences and greater expressions of love. I understood the importance of linear time in the physical realm as a beacon that guides the human consciousness to the exact experience needed for its spiritual expansion. But most importantly of all, in seeing Michael as a physical being, I was able to finally perceive myself as an Angelic being.

The idea of a partnership with Michael was suddenly plausible. He had experience and knowledge of the physical universe, and I felt the infinity and eternity of his. What we share is a Divine Love that exists within all that is.

Unfortunately, within days, I began to lose the awareness and feelings of being an Angelic Being and found myself experiencing life as a human once more. I could no longer see my eternal connections and finally admitted to Michael that I was not worthy of being his partner.

"Little One, we are not asking you to live as an Angel. A partnership between an Angel and a human requires that one of us live as a physical human being on Earth, and in the present situation, that would be you. However, to function as an Angel's partner, you must be whole within yourself, and that requires you to perceive, experience, and express your spiritual energy and your physical being as one."

"That may sound simple to you, Michael, but I have lived my whole life feeling separated from my own Spirit and have no clue how to create wholeness within myself."

"It is easier than you think, Little One. First, you must accept that your Divine Purpose has changed and that this shift offers you many new opportunities to move into wholeness. In the old paradigm, the vibratory frequency of your Spirit was too high to fully enter your physical body.

"This forced your human consciousness to leave your body in order to connect with the Angelic and other realms. You were literally forced to pull your energy out of your crown chakra and speed it up as we in turn lowered our energy to meet it. This process coupled with the Divine Plan of exploring fear, created the belief within you that Spirit is above you and needs to be worshiped, obeyed, and at times even feared. Your misconceptions of Spirit were both loving and necessary in the Old Paradigm, but are now outdated and need to be released. Simply ask and Spirit will remove this belief from you."

That sounded too easy, but I closed my eyes and stated my request. Immediately, I felt a little dizzy, and as Michael continued, I knew my belief systems were already beginning to shift!

"Wholeness simply requires that you offer your willingness to let your Spirit fully enter your physical body. In the beginning, you will need to take a leap of faith and trust that Spirit will never do anything to harm you and will never give you more energy than your physical body can safely handle. We assure you that within a few short days and weeks, your body, mind, and emotions will begin to recognize that Spirit and the physical body are simply individual expressions of the same energy.

"Little One, you think of yourself as having a single vibratory frequency, but in reality your physical being consists of a range of vibratory frequencies. Your physical body is the densest form of your being and therefore moves at the slowest rate. Your thoughts exist at a higher vibratory frequency or speed, and your emotions move even faster. Simply invite your spiritual energy in and watch as it flows through each layer of your being. Your wholeness will automatically begin to manifest on the Earth plane.

"The path to wholeness is an expansion of humanity, not an evolution. The human must retain its unique range of vibratory frequencies even as the Spirit enters. Wholeness can be experienced only when both the human and Spirit contribute fully in each moment. Spirit is entering oneness to share the Earth experience, not to change, take over, or save humanity."

I found this statement disappointing. Michael had been telling me to surrender to Spirit for the last ten years, and now he was telling me that I needed to take responsibility and become its partner. It was very confusing!

"Little One, we are telling you that the Divine Purpose of Earth and every life consciousness on this planet has changed. You and Spirit can now live as one on the Earth plane, but Spirit can only offer you wholeness. You must accept the joining and all that it entails."

Every fiber of my being ached to experience the fulfillment of wholeness, but I had no idea where or how to begin. "Michael, what is my human responsibility in the Spirit/human relationship?"

"ALWAYS DO WHAT IS MOST LOVING FOR YOU!"

"And?"

"And it will be the most loving for every life consciousness around you." That sounded too simple. *"Little One, the difficulty lies in knowing what you really love and what is most loving for you. You have been living in a world of fear, the essence of which is restriction and limitation. Fear has taught you to limit the people you are willing to love to only those that share and mirror your individual fears back to you. Once you create a fear-based relationship, fear demands that you maintain it or lose the love of your life. This forces you to continually focus on what you believe is loving for your partners, children, family members, friends, coworkers, etc in order to provide the love that they need.*

"There is not a life consciousness on Earth that can figure out the Divine Plan of another. You are blessed if you can see even a tiny portion of your own. Trying to fulfill another is impossible. However, taking responsibility for your own fulfillment creates a joy within you that can be shared with all those you truly love, and sharing joy is one of the most loving things that any life consciousness has to offer. When you do what is most loving for you in each situation and mirror all the love you see and feel back to your partner, you begin to create partnerships steeped in Divine Love."

"Michael, how do I discover what is most loving for me?"

"It will take a great deal of focus at first. Allow your physical body to help you with this process. Your body knows what is most loving for you, even when your mind and emotions are confused. Begin with something simple that can be answered with a yes or no. Sit down in a quiet spot, relax, and take three deep breaths. As you ask your question, allow yourself to feel your jaw, back of the neck, shoulder blades, fingers, and the physical sensations in your ascending heart. Once you get a reading on your body, repeat these steps asking the opposite question. A loving statement always creates relaxation and warmth in the body while fear creates tension and coolness.

"We suggest you do not mix in a bunch of conditions; each condition is a different question. Your body can tell you if it is loving to eat chocolate; buy a new car, home, or pair of shoes; walk in the rain; stay in a current relationship or look for a new one. It is also important to remember that the body only functions in the moment. Information about the past and future may be unreliable.

"Your thoughts and emotions can then help to validate the messages from your body. Love is expansive and fulfilling. When your choices are filled only with the energy of love, you will have no doubts or anxiety. If you are unsure or wavering back and forth in your decisions, it is a sign that this is not the loving thing to do in this moment. Wait until your body, mind, and emotions are totally aligned with Spirit, and you will know with total certainty that you are making a loving decision.

"Little One, you are going to be very surprised about what you learn about love and fear in the next few months and years. You will soon find yourself being stripped of fear, withdrawing from old relationships, and changing the groups that you align with. In the Old Paradigm, the individual with the highest vibratory frequency could raise the energy of an entire group. In the New Paradigm, where no one is left behind, the group energy naturally gravitates towards the lowest vibratory frequency in the group. It is a change worth noting.

"Remember, love can only create what is best for you. Don't expect Spirit to support your fear-based efforts any longer, or you will soon be disappointed."

I suddenly realized that learning how to do what is most loving for me could easily take the rest of this lifetime and perhaps a few more. Michael assured me, *"Little One, creating a loving partnership with an Angel or another human is part of the process of becoming whole. You do not have to become whole before you can find a partner. Entering partnerships assists you in the creation of your wholeness. What is the most loving partnership that you can imagine in this moment?"*

It had been ten years since I had even considered the thought of sharing my life with a partner. Shortly after moving to Arizona, I had decided that I should have someone special in my life. I had not been terribly successful in creating relationships in the past, and although I knew what I didn't want, I really had no idea about what I did want. So being the holistic creature that I was, I created list after list trying to describe my soul mate. Frustrated, I finally threw away the lists, went into meditation, and asked the universe to send me a male life-partner that would love me unconditionally. I figured if the human Viki could not attract the perfect man, perhaps Spirit could.

Two weeks later, Spirit guided a male into my life that would unconditionally love me and bring great joy to my life for years to come. That male turned out to be my dog, Buddy, not exactly what I had expected but exactly what I had needed! Now Michael was asking me to reconsider a life partnership.

My mind immediately began to run through its list. I want a partner that adores and loves me unconditionally, someone that I am compatible with and can easily share my space and daily life with. I need someone who will not make me choose between my Angels and him, who will make me feel safe and financially secure, and who will encourage and push me to BE and express absolutely every gift I have been given. My partner needs to be trustworthy, soft, gentle, affectionate, spiritual, and able to love me when I am feeling good about myself and when I am afraid. I want a playmate with a great sense of humor, and a lot of patience, someone willing to take the actions needed to heal Mother Earth. And perhaps most importantly of all, I want someone with a strong desire to provide me with chocolate. The list could go on and on, but I suddenly realized that this was not the heart of the matter.

What I truly desired in a relationship was fulfillment. I needed to BE truly whole as I stood beside my partner, rather than hiding behind the illusions of our entanglements. My heart longed for the freedom to express my love in as many words, forms, feelings, actions, and experiences as I could create.

I wanted to value the love within me so much that I could no longer hold any part of it back from the people and natural world around me. It was time for me to create a place of peace, softness, gentleness, play, and joy on this planet in which all of my relationships could expand. I was ready to step out of the darkness of my planet's fear and into the light that my love shines upon this world.

For years, I had heard Michael say, *"Little One, you must love yourself as you love me,"* and I believed that my love would be worthy of acceptance only when I could love with the purity of an Angel. Only now did I realize that I had added the "must." All those years, Michael had been saying, *"Little One, love yourself as you love me."* I loved Michael as an Angel, and it was time for me to love myself as I am—a loving, fearful human. I am on Earth to express love in human form and that expression of love, whether with an Angel or another human, creates a love that will expand all of creation.

I reached out to the Angel I had grown to know so well, and opened my heart fully to our relationship. I was finally ready to take my vows.

MY PLEDGE

Michael, I love how you wrap your energy around
me, keep me safe, comfort me when I am afraid,
and tell me to *'be afraid, just do it anyway.'*

I love how you refuse to tell me what to do and allow
me the freedom to live my life in my own way, make my
own mistakes, and struggle enough to fully appreciate
the sweetness of my accomplishments both large and
small, and in the process, learn to trust my own choices.

I love that you love Earth's fear and darkness and encourage me to be a happy mess, and that in your presence I no longer desire to strive for the illusions of perfection.

I love asserting my free will, saying no to you, and arguing with you even though I secretly know you are always right.

I love when my actions surprise you, and I love visiting the Angelic Realm and listening in on your conversations with other Angels.

I love to watch as you create new energy that will soon manifest in my world and wonder what it will be and where it will go.

I love that you always do what is best for me. When I am tired, you tell me to rest. When I am excited, you celebrate with me. When I laugh, you enhance my joy. When I am curious, you take me to realms that awe and amaze me. When I wash dishes, you experience the joy of the warm water on my hands. I love knowing there are no moments too small, too silly, or too mundane for you to share with me.

I love that you love me when I cannot love myself.

I love your softness, gentleness, and persistence.

I love looking in the mirror and seeing your blue energy reflected back to me though my own blue eyes.

You are my protector, my friend, my playmate, my teacher, my guardian, my healer, and my inspiration.

Standing beside you, I feel loved, fulfilled, whole, and powerful.

From this day forward, I pledge to walk the Earth
with you, and openly and freely express my love
for you to every life consciousness on Earth.

chapter twenty-seven

Falling In Love

Falling in love is Earth's greatest gift!

It is the moment when two beings suddenly remember the soul that stands before them and find the courage to leave all their fears and doubts behind. It is the moment when two beings finally gaze into each other's eyes and express their true feelings to each other, and simply allow the sweet softness of their essences to flow freely into one another. In that moment, each individual is totally fulfilled as love is both given and received! Falling in love exists only in a moment of timelessness.

Staying in the timelessness of Divine Love is much more difficult; fear would have you believe it is impossible! Perhaps that is because all of our Old Paradigm relationships were created to mirror fear back to our partner and this often required the use of time. Many individuals continue to fall out of love not because of what is happening in the moment, but because of what has happened in the past or what they fear will happen in the future. To truly share love across the time of our planet one must live in the moment.

Michael always says, *"There is no such thing as committing to a long-term relationship. The choice to share your life with another happens in each moment. The length of a partnership can be measured only in the shared experiences of your past, not the future. Love is rarely lost in the moment. It is forgotten through living in the past and future."*

I had just expressed my Divine Love to Michael and agreed to expand our relationship. In the past, we had shared many different types of partnerships. There was the channeling, in which my human mind stepped aside and let Michael take over. Then there was the relationship we shared within my magical bubbles, in which both my mental and emotional energy aligned and allowed my physical and spiritual energy to take center stage. However, Michael was now asking for a very different type of relationship, one that could only be created in each moment through the expression of love.

Somewhere deep within my consciousness was the awakening knowledge of what it meant to live in the fulfillment of love rather than the fear of loss, but I had no idea how to use this information to create the partnership I truly desired. I have never met another human who has openly admitted to having an Angel as a life partner (although I'm pretty sure there are more of you out there), so I turned to Michael for the next step in my journey.

"Little One, in order to express Divine Love, your physical being must be in synchronicity. Synchronicity simply means that you are thinking, feeling, saying, and doing the same thing in each moment. Very few people on Earth have achieved this state. In fact, fear is dependent on the ability to multitask and deceive others by hiding your thoughts and feelings behind your words and actions.

"However, you will soon find that synchronicity creates a wholeness within you that is calm and peaceful, and that allows your spiritual love to smoothly flow through every layer of your being with little or no resistance. This process takes practice, so be patient, it may take a little time to create this new habit, but once accomplished, fear will soon be left behind.

"Once you have achieved the ability to move your energy

through your body in synchronicity, you will discover that you can also experience your outer world with the same ease. In the Old Paradigm, humans often primarily focused on only one aspect of their experiences at a time. The intellectual immediately began thinking about what was happening, the emotional individual responded to what they were feeling, and the physical person took action. Only after the primary response was satisfied were the other aspects of one's being allowed to react to the situation. The complete human experience of any single event could occur in a few moments, days, weeks, or even years.

"This process of separating and drawing out an experience over time was created to prevent humanity from being totally overwhelmed by the experiences of fear. However, in the synchronicity of the Angelic Movement, one's experiences are created with love, and no one needs to be protected from love. Individuals can now safely experience all their thoughts, feelings, and actions in each moment, bringing a new depth and beauty to life on Earth. Synchronicity expands your ability to experience life in each moment and in so doing, expands each of you into the wholeness of your being."

I began to practice this process and soon discovered that it was the hardest thing I had ever tried to do. I had to face how often I hid my feelings from others and judged my thoughts as unworthy of being expressed. Now I am not saying that every thought and feeling that I had should have been blurted out—that's the last thing this world needed—but paying attention to my thoughts, feelings, and actions in each moment really showed me how much negativity I carried around with me, and how inconsistently I manifested my love in the physical world.

I had been asking Michael to remove my unwanted thoughts and feelings for almost a year, but suddenly, stripping them away became his full-time job! Luckily, he actually seemed to enjoy it and within a few months, I was feeling physically lighter, more mentally alert, and very calm and peaceful. I found myself less irritated with the craziness of the world as my sense of humor rapidly increased! I was actually beginning to enjoy living on this planet.

"It's time to go into Sacred Space, Little One." I wasn't sure why Michael wanted me to go into Sacred Space, but Pink Lady, Green Guy, Orange, and Yellow were lined up in a straight row to greet me when I arrived.

Pink Lady reached out and took my hand. *"We have someone for you to meet."* Green Guy, Orange, and Yellow quickly stepped aside, revealing a huge white Angel sitting a few yards away. As Pink Lady guided me towards her, a gentle breeze caressed my face, arms, and hands, and a rush of sweetness filled my entire body.

She was at least fifteen feet tall with soft white hair that fell to her waist. Her eyes were a piercing ice blue, and her skin was the color of pure white snow glistening with a thousand tiny, rainbow-colored ice crystals embedded within its surface. Her dress and boots were made of soft white fur, but it was her wings that made the greatest impression. They were massive and extended from well above her head to her ankles. The wings contained thousands of white feathers of various sizes and shapes, and when she spread them outward, they encircled not only me, but Pink Lady, Green Guy, Orange, and Yellow as well.

"Little One, I am White. I am the Angel that you are. I am the Divine Love that continuously flows through all your soul essences, creating your physical being and the substance of all that you are and need to experience on the physical plane. I am your connection to the universal knowledge of the Angelic Realm. No longer will you be required to enter our realm through Michael's energy field in order to maintain your safety. I bring you the choice to enter our realm in the wholeness of your Angelic/human connection and stand beside Michael in both realms as a true partner.

"I have come to create the life of love that you are now ready to experience on this planet. I bring the oneness and infinity of the Angelic Realm into your life so you may see the Earth and its

experiences as those in the Angelic Realm perceive it. I ask permission to integrate my energy into your thoughts, emotions, and physical body and guide you into the expression of love on the Earth plane.

"I ask to share your life, in peace and with the gift of freedom from intrusion. The free will to choose fear will never be interrupted, the mind overridden, the emotions dismissed, or the body prevented from taking action. I come to BE a part of you through the next stage of your journey. Once integrated into your physical being, you may have difficulty feeling my essence, but know I am always within you. Pink Lady will remain your dominant personality and conduct the day-to-day business of your life; I simply offer you wholeness by bringing the eternal love that you are into your physical being.

As I leaned into White, she gently pulled me close and wrapped her arms around me. Then with a few silent beats of her wings, we were flying above the valley floor and soon passed Blue as he stood atop his favorite mountain peak. We paused for a moment on a fluffy white cloud and then White wrapped her wings around me, stepped off the cloud, and began to spin faster and faster as we plummeted back to Earth. By the time my feet touched the valley floor, White was inside of me and I was breathless and giddy from falling in love with my eternal soul!

chapter twenty-eight

Heaven And Earth

"Welcome to *Heaven and Earth* with Viki Hart and Archangel Michael, where we celebrate the connections between humans and Angels! You are listening to TellerNetcast.com, your local Internet news, talk, and culture."

Shortly after returning from opening the two doorways in October of 2008, Amy Elmont, a close friend and coworker at Celebration, asked me to be a guest on her metaphysical radio show, *The Lighter Side*. We talked about the Earth changes that were occurring as well as my work with Angels. I was very nervous, but Amy made me comfortable and it was a lot of fun, so several months later when Amy created her own parenting show and approached me to take over *The Lighter Side*, I said yes.

We decided to change the name of the show and add Archangel Michael to the mix. The station was in a very conservative community and the idea of talking to Angels was, to say the least, a little outside of the normal conversation. However, the station was new, I was volunteering my services, very few people were listening and the owner of the station was open minded, so *Heaven and Earth* put Archangel Michael on the air.

Each week, we would interview a local metaphysical practitioner and Michael would channel an Angelic view of our topic while throwing in a few comments about what was happening in the world around us. To help the show run more smoothly, Michael would channel his segment to me in advance, sometimes before we had even booked the guest.

The shows were diverse and amazing, and in spite of the fact that I did all the pre-show interviews and chose the questions for our guests, Michael was in charge. Most of my questions went unasked as Michael guided us in unexpected directions, and the more spontaneous things became, the better the shows were. It seemed that Michael had taken my pledge to walk the Earth with him and to openly and freely proclaim my love for him to every life consciousness on Earth very seriously!

After the first few shows, it became evident that Michael had things he wanted to say about the global process of the Angelic Movement. In the past, we had focused on the interests and concerns of individuals and small groups, but as Michael began to reveal the larger patterns of energy around us, the chaos and destruction in our world revealed a new more benevolent purpose. Michael was teaching us not only about energy, he was teaching us about who we really are and how to use our energy in new ways.

Michael began by describing energy waves. He had been telling me for years that the Angelic Movement was simply about moving the energy of the Angelic Realm into the physical universe in order to create a new world of love. However, for the past few years, I had envisioned waves of Divine Love being pushed into the Earth in the same way that a soul enters the body at conception. I had just assumed that the Angelic Realm was responsible for the amount and timing of the waves, but suddenly Michael was showing me that it is the physical world that is creating these waves.

"Little One, the energy of the Angelic Realm needs a physical conduit through which to enter your planet. This conduit can be a

human, animal, plant, crystal, molecule of air or water, etc. Each time a life consciousness on Earth expresses love, more of their individualized spiritual energy is pulled into the physical realm. As the energy of love is expressed to the outer world, it begins to expand and join in oneness with all other expressions of love. This process creates a wave that flows around your planet, touching every life consciousness along the way.

"Over the past few years, humanity has also discovered that large groups of people leaving the Earth at the same time can join to create a wave by sending a final gift of love back to Earth from the veil between our realms."

"Michael, are these waves the sensations I have been feeling after the Earthquakes and tsunamis of the past few years?"

"Yes, Little One, and expect more of this type of wave in the future. In fact, more humans are deciding to leave the Earth in large groups in order to offer those they leave behind this great gift of love.

"These new energy waves of love cannot support your fears. As you have previously seen with the pink fizz, the higher energy of love actually dissolves the lower energy of fear upon contact. So as the energy of love is increasing on your planet, the lower vibratory frequencies of fear are disappearing.

"Your planet has learned from past attempts that the balance of energy on your physical planet must be maintained in order to prevent the physical destruction of both the natural world and human culture. While we of the Angelic Realm perceive the expansion of love on your planet, humanity is currently experiencing the unraveling of fear's creations.

"As the first individual life consciousness on Earth began to move into the new energy in 2007, there was not enough Angelic energy to even create a wave. While each consciousness was able to maintain its own life path, there was very little one could do but stand by and watch the world of fear begin to fall apart. However, by the beginning

of 2008, twenty percent of the consciousness of Earth had chosen to move into the new energy and the first large waves began appearing approximately every three months.

"Much of this energy was coming through the natural world and occurred on the winter and summer solstices and the spring and fall equinoxes. The higher energy of love expands at a very rapid rate."

The following table of dates and equations illustrates the movement of energy that Michael was describing:

YEAR	% IN NEW ENERGY	INCREASE IN LOVE BASED ENERGY	DECREASE IN FEAR BASED ENERGY
2008	20	2^2 = 4 TIMES	1/2 OF ORIGINAL AMOUNT
2009	40	4^4 = 256 TIMES	1/4 OF ORIGINAL AMOUNT
2010	60	6^6 = 46,656 TIMES	1/6 OF ORIGINAL AMOUNT
2011	80	8^8 = 16,777,216 TIMES	1/8 OF ORIGINAL AMOUNT

It was becoming very clear to me that the energy of the Angelic Movement would very quickly expand to the amount needed to begin the creation of a new world. The strange thing was that I had no idea what this new world would look like, how big it would be, or where we were going to put it. I mean, were the two worlds going to occupy the same space, sit side by side, overlap each other, exist in two different reams, melt into each other, or what?

"Get out of your head, Little One. Your new world will be created from your Spirit, not your mind. As one world dissolves away, the other will take its place. Just as your body has a range of vibratory frequencies that make up your whole, the planet also consists of a range of vibratory frequencies. During 2007 and 2008, the Angelic energy entering your planet most closely matched the frequencies of

Earth's mental energy. Therefore, manifestations that were created with fear through the thoughts and ideas of humans began to fall apart.

"This continuing shift will result in the collapse of many more fear-based manifestations throughout the next few years, forcing fear, which has previously been hidden from view, to rise to the surface in an attempt to maintain what is left of its creations. Many more individuals will find they can longer deny and repress their deepest fears, and even institutions created in fear will be opened to public scrutiny.

"As the energy of love continues to expand on the Earth plane, additional frequencies will be added. 2009 will add the vibratory frequencies most closely related to the emotional energy of the physical plane, so relationships and other forms of emotional manifestations will begin to be effected on a planetary level. Relationships based only in fear will begin to dissolve, as fear based-patterns of behavior become ineffective in holding a relationship together.

"Control and manipulation will lose their power as love shines its light on each individual's hidden fears and agendas, bringing them to the surface to be released. As this occurs, it may actually appear as if there is more fear and destruction in the world. Let us assure you that only fear is being lost.

"The magic of this time lies in each individual's choice to use energy waves to speed up their own spiritual process. Little One, each time you release a fear, you now let it go forever, and each time you express your Divine Love on the planet, you create a new pattern of love that will expand your consciousness forever! The Angelic energy within you and the Angelic waves flowing back towards you are completely compatible. As you continuously release the lower energies of fear from your physical being, the Angelic energy within you rises to meet the Angelic energy coming towards you, and as they join in oneness all the love in your life begins to expand.

"However, if you choose to hold onto your fears and their

manifestations, the higher energy waves in the outer world can overrun you and may even seem to knock you off your feet. Those humans that are still in fear may feel as if they are drowning or suffocating as the energy presses down on them.

"By the beginning of 2010, the energy of the Angelic Movement will expand its range to include those vibratory frequencies most closely related to the physical body. This expansion will bring to the surface all old physical injuries, illnesses, and diseases which need to be cleared from the physical body in order to allow the expanded spiritual energy to flow freely through you. It is important for you to remember that once energy is manifested physically, it must be dealt with physically. Pay attention to those aches and pains that you have been ignoring for years.

"Little One, you are not getting older, you are creating the foundation of your new body. If you need antibiotics, take them. If you need a massage, get one. If you need a tooth filled, have it done. If you want to lose ten pounds, do so. Let go of what you do not want in your body and allow all the strength and wellness of Spirit to manifest."

As Michael spoke about the effects of the waves on our physical bodies, I suddenly realized that my body was reacting to the waves with headaches and diarrhea. I wanted to start manifesting love, not discomfort, so I asked Michael to show me how to rise and meet the waves. Michael asked me to sit down in my rocking chair, close my eyes, relax, and take three deep breaths.

"Little One, imagine that a beautiful deep blue wave is coming towards you. The wave is at least three times your height and is filled with golden rays of light streaming upwards from the base of the wave and flowing over its crest. As is approaches, simply relax and go with the flow. Let the golden rays of light pull you up the face of the wave and gently deposit you on its foamy top. Once there, simply allow your body to ride the wave wherever it may take you."

I did as Michael instructed and suddenly felt the huge wave

beneath me racing across a large body of open water. Suddenly, the wave gently deposited me in a large padded seat with a bar across the front. Immediately, I felt myself falling and knew from the dizziness in my head and the excited thrill of my stomach that I was on a gigantic Ferris wheel!

As my seat continued to descend, I moved through the yellow spray of a sunlit waterfall and into the Earth itself. I rejoiced as the Ferris wheel took me through the familiar energy of the crystalline structure and moved me backwards through the molten core of the Earth. Soon we began to ascend and I found myself surrounded by ice, only to break free of its grip and soar towards a deep blue sky. I loved Ferris wheels, so I made a few more rotations before I asked, "Where am I?"

Instantly, White was beside me. She wrapped her arms around me. As our seat reached its highest point, she pulled me upward to the very edge of our planet. From the boundary of space, I turned and looked back to see the continent of Australia and the islands of New Zealand below me.

"Little One, you have two more doorways to open!"

chapter twenty-nine

Humanity's Greatest Gift

The land down under has fired my imagination since childhood. Exotic animals with even more exotic names like Kangaroo, Koala Bear, Emu, Wombat, Duck-Billed Platypus, and Tasmanian Devil, all living on the other side of the world, drew me to a land so alien from my Illinois farm town that it might as well have been the moon. When Michael had announced that Blue was ready to go home, my only unfulfilled dream was visiting this wondrous land. It now appeared that even this elusive dream was about to be brought to life!

I immediately got on my computer and began looking for waterfalls in Australia. I soon discovered that not only is the continent of Australia exotic, it is very large and has hundreds of waterfalls. It took me about a week to go through the territories one by one, looking for waterfalls that matched the one I had seen on my Ferris wheel ride. I was able to narrow the list down to New South Wales and Tasmania, but still had seven waterfalls that fit both my vision and the characteristics of the previous doorways.

I was stumped, and while trying to solve this mystery on my own really was fun, it was time to ask Michael for a hint. Michael showed me a small pink pig and asked me to think bigger! It was a very cute pig and somehow familiar, but in a land filled with exotic animals, these clues seemed to be of no help whatsoever. However, this was the adventure of a lifetime and no farm animal was going to get in my way!

Then late one night, I found a reference for a video of an Australian waterfall on YouTube and clicked on it. The video was of a young couple with a waterfall in the background. I could see only a portion of the waterfall behind them, but the roar of the water immediately pulled my consciousness into it and I knew that Carrington Falls was the site of my next doorway.

While this waterfall was in New South Wales, I had not previously considered it because it was twice the height of the Colorado, Wales, and Peru falls. As I began to search for more information on Carrington Falls, I discovered that it was just outside the small town of Robertson, which is best known as an agricultural center and the film site for the movie *Babe,* which coincidently is about a pig.

Once I discovered the site of the Australian doorway, it was time to look for the New Zealand site. I again started looking for waterfalls and found that while the islands of New Zealand are small, they are filled with some of the most beautiful waterfalls in the world. I screened each waterfall that I could find in New Zealand without feeling a single connection. After a few frustrated days, I relaxed and began to simply look at every breathtaking picture I could find.

There were mountains, beaches, forests, lakes, green valleys, and then suddenly right in front of me were the glaciers! The Ferris wheel had brought me up through the ice and into the blue sky. The New Zealand doorway was not behind a waterfall, it was beneath the ice, and just like Molasses Reef, we were going to pull the energy up through the water—this water just happened to be frozen!

Once I discovered the sites of the new matrixes, I was so excited that I just wanted to get on a plane and head west. However, there were a few problems, such as when Mother Earth would be ready to accept the new energy and how to finance this trip, which would cost almost four times the amount of money that I had available. So I turned to my partner in all things spiritual and asked Michael what to do next.

"Little One, these two matrixes are much larger than anything we have attempted before. We need to prepare your physical body to handle this additional energy. In order to do so, we suggest you set up a seminar at Mt. Princeton where you will open a temporary doorway and hold it open for a small group of people for twenty-four hours. In addition, you will visit and use the energy of Agnes Vaille Falls to increase your physical vibratory frequency. Depending on how your body reacts, we will open the doorways sometime after Christmas."

I immediately called Mt. Princeton Resort, which books all its events a year in advance, and found that a group had cancelled their event that morning and that the second weekend in July was available. During the next six weeks, Michael and I channeled all the information for the seminar, put together all the activities, written materials, music, food, and found a group of ten participants. It was a whirlwind of activity that was both fun and easy, but left no time for me to dwell on the fact that I had never done anything like this before and really didn't know what I was doing.

We began the seminar by opening a temporary doorway in the conference center, and while Michael and I had opened matrixes for classes in the past, this experience was very different. The moment this doorway opened, I was not only in my magical bubble, I was able to invite the participants in as well. It was the most fun I had ever had in my life! I felt so physically close to Michael that I could almost see him standing beside me, and his voice was so clear that I sometimes forgot that the other people in the room could not hear him.

The group went to Agnes Vaille Falls on the first day. It was cloudy and sprinkling on and off during our time at the falls, and there were moments when the doorway actually appeared to be lit from within. While the energies of the four doorways flowed in and out of each other, each section of the trail was dominated by one of these vibratory frequencies, and it was fun to see which matrix different individuals were most comfortable with.

As I stood back and watched each individual unconsciously react to the changes in the energy around them, I began to understand how the Divine Plan made room for every life consciousness on the planet. As each doorway was opened, its unique vibratory frequency of love was added to the planet, and this new energy served to connect the diverse expressions of love on Earth. Oneness really is the totality of our individual expressions of love!

That evening, we introduced the upcoming shift in the power grid of our planet. All life consciousnesses of Earth combine their individual energies to create our physical world. Think of each individual consciousness as connected into a power plant by both an input and output line. Each individual sends its energy into the power plant, which then creates and maintains our shared physical world. All excess energy is then made available for additional individual manifestations.

This grid worked well for many millennia until fear began to convince humanity that there was an energy shortage, and more and more individuals began to limit their energy input, take out more than they needed and even offer a lower quality of energy to the plant. In time, the power plant began to break down and run much less efficiently, and the natural world began to suffer.

The energy of the Angelic Movement will not be used to repair, maintain, or increase the output of the old power plant; in fact, the energies of the two power plants are incompatible. The new power grid will be created to handle the higher vibratory frequency of love. For example, if the old power lines delivered 110 volts, the new plant will offer 500 volts. Each individual life consciousness will be required to unplug from the old plant before plugging into the new energy source. Fear-based individuals and groups will no longer have an effect on those connected to the new grid, and those in the new grid will no longer be able to support fear-based manifestations.

Michael explained, *"The moment on Earth in which Divine Love begins its expression and creation is upon you. The new power plant and grid have already been manifested on the Earth plane and will automatically activate when the percentage of life consciousnesses in the Angelic Movement reaches fifty percent. A short time later, as the consciousness of love reaches fifty-one percent, it will take over the physical manifestation of your world.*

"The old grid will remain online for as long as there are individual consciousnesses that need it, but expect problems as the energy input begins to rapidly diminish and the system continues to fall apart. There may be times when very little energy is available through the old system and even individual manifestations of fear will come to a halt."

An hour later, following a group meditation designed to open the participants to the use of the new energy grid, a sudden sense of calm and peace began to permeate the room. One of the participants smiled and exclaimed, "The energy of the room just shifted!"

To this, Michael responded, *"The energy of the planet just shifted!"* It was the evening of July 11, 2009. Michael had brought me back to Mt. Princeton to witness the activation of the power of love exactly three years to the day of opening our first Angelic Doorway at Agnes Vaille Falls.

A few weeks after the seminar, I was sitting in my living room watching Buddy play with his dog treats when Michael asked me to go into Sacred Space. I went into meditation and was immediately greeted by White, who informed me that we were going into the Angelic Realm. I had only entered the Angelic Realm without Michael once before, in November of 1995, and the results had been disastrous, so I was more than a little hesitant. White was aware of my fear and continued to assure me that it would be both easy and comfortable, and I soon agreed.

However, from the moment I entered the Angelic Realm, I knew something had changed! I was still able to fly and was acutely aware of both my individualized strand and oneness in the Angelic Realm, but I was also aware of everything that was happening on Earth. This ability to experience both realms at the same time was completely new to me.

As I settled into the wonder of this new way of experiencing, I began to feel the energy within and around me begin to gain speed and intensity. I was aware of Ariella, Uriel, Gabriel, and Raphael near me and I reached out for Michael. Suddenly, I felt his energy expanding in the area of the Angelic Realm that contained the physical universe. In the same moment, I was aware of my physical body sitting in my rocking chair.

As Michael's energy reached out to completely surround the planet, I felt his energy pass between my feet and Mother Earth. My human mind immediately interpreted this action as Archangel Michael taking his sword and severing my connection with Mother Earth.

As the energy of the Angelic Realm began to return to its previous state, I asked Michael what had just happened. *"In the beginning of the Earth experience, humanity agreed to be the primary creator of fear on the planet. In return, Mother Earth agreed to take many of the fears and toxins created within the human body into her larger body. These human fears and toxins would be deposited deep within Mother Earth's fossil fuels and heavy metals. Humans would then offer their love to Mother Earth and its higher energy would be added to these depositories.*

"Over thousands of years, the energy of love would dissolve these fears and toxins. This system would allow humans to maintain the state of physical health needed to complete their Divine Paths within their relatively short life spans.

"This system worked for many generations until humanity created the collective belief that it was separate and above the natural world. This belief resulted in many humans withholding their love from Mother Earth while still dumping their fears and toxins into her.

This process has intensified over the last few thousand years until the present day, in which Mother Earth is completely overwhelmed with the lower energies of fear. In addition, many of the Earth's fossil fuels have been removed from the ground, exacerbating the problem as large amounts of humanity's past fears and negativity are released on the surface of the planet. The planet is very ill and having difficulty maintaining her own functions.

"The collective consciousness of love has reached fifty-one percent and its first manifestation has been to create a safe haven for Mother Earth to begin her healing. The connection, which allowed humans to release their fears and toxins into the Earth, has just been severed. While this action will greatly ease the pain of the planet, humans will now need to create new ways of dealing with their fears and toxins in order to remain comfortable and healthy. This manifestation was completed with the full understanding of its ramifications for the human race, and in so doing, has become the greatest gift humanity has ever been given!"

chapter thirty

A Promise Kept

"Let Viki try it, she'll try anything."
I was eavesdropping on the Angelic Realm. My new connection with White allowed me to listen in on the Angelic Realm without entering it, and while much of the activity of the realm made no sense to me or was boring (meaning it had nothing to do with me), every now and then a true gem of information caught my attention. This was one of those times.

I had often accused Michael of using me as a guinea pig in the manifestation of the Angelic Movement on Earth, and I was convinced that I finally had the proof that my theory was correct! *"There is a risk; she may not be ready to handle the energy."* Maybe I was wrong; I recognized that last statement as Michael's energy.

"It is still the softest option and it is her path; we must offer her the choice."

Several days later, I was walking in the park with Buddy when Michael said, *"We need to talk."* I sat down in the shade of my favorite tree and Buddy came and lay down beside me. *"Little One, we had hoped to open the Australia and New Zealand doorways after the increase in Angelic energy that will enter the physical realm on the winter solstice of this year. However, the recent decisions made by humanity to place the health of the Earth above that of humans has changed many things on your planet. While this is the most loving thing that humanity has ever done, it has placed into motion a series of events that could be catastrophic to areas inhabited by large numbers of humans. These actions were planned and are a necessary part of the process of healing the planet, but they have been moved up in linear time by humanity's decisions.*

"Mother Earth is now able to begin her healing immediately and this includes shifting of tectonic plates, volcanic activity, and changes in weather patterns all designed to release fear, toxins, and stress from her physical body. Mother Earth is aware that the change in the timetable of her healing will leave many of her children unaware of what is about to happen, which will limit their ability to make an informed choice as to the path they wish to take.

"The One Soul of Earth has devised several options to deal with the physical changes of the planet. The assistance of approximately one hundred humans will be needed over the next few months, and the Australian and New Zealand doorways are an integral part of the plan. We know you are committed to these doorways, but you must understand that there is a risk that you are not yet ready to handle the energy within these matrixes. We want you to talk to your body and your soul essences before you make a decision."

Over the next week, I had several discussions with my physical body and soul essences. My physical body was aware of the matrixes that had been created within it and seemed to really enjoy them. The concern was that the amount of energy that would flow through me as the doorways were being opened was too great for my physical body to safely handle.

Green Guy, the healer of the group, suggested we anchor the cylinder in place and then step out of it before the doorway was opened. We could then open a link from my ascending heart chakra and join the matrix within my body to the matrix in the natural world.

This would still allow my physical energy to activate the doorway from this side while lessening the amount of energy flowing directly through my body. The Angelic Realm agreed that this method of opening the doorway would be much safer and would accomplish the task.

"Little One, even though this method is safer than pulling the energy directly through your body, there is still a risk. You must enter each matrix with a completely open heart. Any conscious or unconscious fears that lie within you could be manifested during the linkage."

"Michael, if I do this and something does go wrong, will I have completed my Divine Path in this lifetime?"

"Yes, Little One, the risk is not life threatening, but it could endanger your ability to create future matrixes."

"I have dreamed of Australia all my life. If I had only one gift to give the world, this doorway would be it. I really want to do this, Michael."

"We have three weeks to prepare, Little One."

I am completely aware that our manifestations in the outer world always reflect our inner needs, desires, and fears, so I was not surprised when I suddenly panicked over my finances. My fear of not being able to handle the energy of the doorways had quickly manifested into my anxiety about how to pay for this trip. The seminar had provided me with less than half the amount I needed and there was no time to set up additional classes.

I struggled with taking a leap of faith that if I used my credit cards, I would be able to pay them off in the future. I knew that if I could not pay at least the minimum amount each month, I risked losing my home. The trip may not have been life threatening, but since I worked out of my home and was risking my job as well, a financial death seemed possible. I had a week of sleepless nights begging Spirit to help me.

Then one night, I awoke at two in the morning in a state of

complete peace and serenity. I got on the computer and booked airline flights, hotels, and rental cars before I went back to bed and slept until noon. During the following week, I made arrangements to take a glacier tour in New Zealand and was asked to work four extra days at Celebration. I had my spending money and was ready to go.

My life was very hectic in those last three weeks as I worked extra hours, made arrangements for Buddy, procured my Visa, read the "Rules of the Road" for both Australia and New Zealand, and wondered if I really could drive on the left side of the road. I had taken months to prepare for my previous overseas trips, but thanks to humanity's sudden change of heart, I had no choice but to live in the moment, laugh, and just do whatever was in front of me in each moment.

Yet through it all, I continued to feel a sense of great urgency in the Angelic Realm. The week prior to my leaving the states, Sydney was hit with a red dust storm and the televised reports showed a city that appeared to be on fire as all flights in and out were cancelled. The nearby island of Samoa was hit by a huge earthquake and suffered a great deal of damage and loss of life. Finally, I stopped, took a deep breath, and asked Michael what was happening.

"Little One, the recent shift in the consciousness of the One Soul of Earth is beginning to manifest in the physical realm. The tectonic plates of the Pacific Rim are becoming unstable. The concern is that as the larger plates begin to shift, they will cause a cascading effect across the Pacific Ocean and beyond. This is similar to what occurred in the fall of Atlantis when the Atlantic rim collapsed as its plates began to flip.

"The spiritual plan of Earth is to use energy from the Angelic Realm to stabilize the plates. We will draw Angelic energy from the doorway in Australia into the core of the Earth, then pull it up through the glacier in New Zealand and join it with the doorway in Australia to make a ring. As the plates begin to shift, the ring of energy will

allow the plates to move up and down but not flip, localizing the quakes." This reminded me of my Ferris wheel meditation!

"This process will be repeated in many different areas of the Pacific in the next few days and weeks, and possibly around the planet in the near future. The planet is so toxic and damaged at the present time that the Earth must use all its healing techniques to survive, but the mother loves her children and wants to make this process as gentle and soft as possible."

I could feel the love not only in Michael's words, but flowing beneath my feet as well. I had promised Mother Earth in Wales that I would find a way to save her and us. I was ready to keep that promise by risking everything that I was, everything that I had, and everything that might be to do just that!

chapter thirty-one

Carrington Falls

Human Being—the first time I remember hearing this phrase was as a small child when I asked my family, "Who am I?" Even as a three-year-old, I was striving for an esoteric explanation of life. Unfortunately, the rest of the world did not share my need to remember that we are Spirit as well as physical, and went about their business of making me into the best little human being I could be.

I eventually complied with the wishes of my world, but not before creating an obsessive need to control every aspect of my life. With only three weeks to prepare for my trip, there had been no time to think about—let alone try to control—my situation. I merely moved from one activity to another and somehow everything, including the laundry, got done.

This had been an unusual experience for me. Usually I made three or four lists and still stopped to review each one before deciding what I needed to do next. The actions that created this trip were guided by intuition rather than thought, and it gave a whole new meaning to the term human being. I had learned to associate being human with my conscious mind, as if my existence was solely dependent on what I thought and did in the physical world.

However, in the last few weeks, I had been guided by my silent inner knowing. My daily existence as a Spirit/human had been brought forth out of necessity, but I soon found this mode of being quite efficient as well as easy and fun. By the time I had dropped Buddy off at his doggy resort and was putting my clothes in the suitcase, I had become quite comfortable with allowing the Spirit within to guide all of my actions. My magical bubble had not only returned, but also appeared to be here to stay!

My neighbor took me to the airport and, as usual, I got through check-in and security in less than fifteen minutes. I had plenty of time to eat breakfast and take in the beautiful view of Pikes Peak before heading to my gate. There I ran into my friend and healer, Marsha Sterling, who was on the same flight to LAX. There was no one on this planet who had done more to help me prepare for this adventure, and I thanked Spirit for allowing us to share a few minutes of awe, wonder, and excitement as my lifetime dream began to unfold.

The night flight from LAX to Sydney was both long and wonderful. After dinner, I settled in and was able to sleep for almost eight hours, awakening to a hot breakfast and a 6:30 am arrival on the other side of the world. It never ceases to amaze me how our human technology has made every inch of Mother Earth so easily accessible.

The magic of my trip continued as I rented a car and found that driving on the left side of the road seemed natural to me. There were times when I actually felt like I was driving in Colorado, and then I would come over a hill and see the soft blue ocean off to my left, the miles of gum trees lining the road and I knew I had landed in Oz. As I headed inland, the gently rolling fields and pastures filled with sheep and cattle reminded me of my own childhood home.

That is, until I hit the curves of Illawarar Highway and began to quickly climb towards the town of Robertson. I took a few wrong turns and at one point was greeted by a large number of very loud geese, but the people were kind and directed me to Rose Ella Bed and Breakfast. My host and his dog were warm and friendly, and after helping me get settled in, he gave me directions to several waterfalls, local sites, and eating establishments.

I had planned to rest for a while, but Michael immediately asked me to change clothes and head for the falls. *"There is a storm moving in and we need to release the matrix this afternoon."*

I changed, grabbed my crystal, and arrived at the trailhead less than twenty minutes later. It was an easy five-minute walk to the falls, and I could feel its pull on my body as I got out of the car. Storm clouds were beginning to fill the sky and as it started sprinkling, people began leaving the area. I was left alone on a trail that was densely lined with a wide variety of blooming trees, bushes, and flowers, all of which seemed to be enjoying the onset of spring. As I came around a small bend and saw Carrington Falls for the first time, I stopped in my tracks and clung to the railing before me. I was standing at the edge of a 160-foot sheer drop into Kangaroo Valley!

In contrast to the open cultivated fields that lay less than a mile away, the energy of this place was immense, primal, and it spoke to me of the upheaval and violence that had created it. A few hundred yards to my right, a massive rock cliff spanned the valley wall. I could hear and see the rush of water as it approached and threw itself over the edge in a deliberate downward flight of fancy. The water fell in two large ribbons of glistening white that joined into a single strand about a third of the way down the falls.

The walls of the gorge were alive with trees and vegetation, and from my viewpoint, I was unable to see the base of the falls and valley floor. As I looked to my left, the valley disappeared into the mist. Human beings were outsiders here, for it is doubtful that man even existed when this place was created. I knew in my heart that there was nothing that man has or will ever conceive of having that could match the natural power and beauty of this place. I felt small and completely unnoticed by the consciousness that flowed around me.

I walked along the trail towards the falls and at one point was able to see a small dark pool of water that lay 164 feet below the top. I realized that it would be impossible for me to open the matrix from the base of the falls as I had previously done.

Michael said, *"We will open this matrix from the top of the falls,"* and then guided me to another trail that exited the woods just beyond the cliff. As I neared the bank of the Kangaroo River, I stopped to pick up a stick to use in releasing the matrix and noticed that every rock in the area was yellow. I had to laugh as I remembered the yellow flickers coming out of the water on my Ferris wheel ride. I thanked Michael and the Universe for again validating that I was indeed in the right place to open a matrix.

I sat down on a large flat rock a few yards beyond the safety rail and about two feet from the edge of the cliff. I really like heights, but the water rushing past me made me a little dizzy and sitting down made me feel much more secure. Michael then asked me to release the matrix, and so with my crystal and stick, I opened each chakra and surrendered to the power and presence of God within me.

I felt a sudden surge of heat rise from every cell of my body and watched as its yellow energy spilled out of my chest and flowed over the edge of the cliff. Then it disappeared and I felt a twinge of disappointment—I had not seen the matrix take form as in the past. Michael quickly assured me that the matrix was so large that it would take some time to physically form, and we would return to open the doorway in a few days. For now, it was time to go before the storm reached our location.

I went into Robertson and ate before I returned to the Bed and Breakfast. Everywhere I stopped, people were friendly and helpful. I just wanted to sit and soak in the local atmosphere and listen to the people talk. I had always loved British and Australian accents and quickly learned that accents in Australia vary as much as those in the United States. By the time I fell into bed that night, I had lost a day in time and was halfway through the ritual that had brought me to this place.

I awoke the next morning to the sound of heavy wind and rain, which I soon discovered was also forecast for tomorrow, so Michael suggested I relax and get some rest. That evening, I met a couple from Sydney at the Bed and Breakfast who were going shopping in a nearby town the next day and I tagged along with them. Their daughter had just spent a week in Colorado Springs so we had a lot to share. We shopped, stopped at a local pub, hung out at the railroad station and museum, and sampled the local cuisine. We returned to the warmth of Rose Ella's fireplace, high tea, and wonderful conversation.

My hosts were saddened that I was spending my holiday in the rain, but I felt as though I was discovering the real Australia in the hearts of its people. Everyone I met was eager to share the stories of their lives and the love of their land with me, and I was honored and humbled by the kindness and consideration I observed in the everyday lives of farmers, butchers, storekeepers, teachers, and others. There is an intimate connection between Australians that reminded me of the people of Wales. People look at one another and really mean it when they ask, "How may I help you?"

On Monday, October 5, 2009, I returned to Carrington Falls. It was early morning, the birds were singing, and the sun was finally shining. Michael took me to the opposite side of the gorge and led me down a trail in the forest. After about twenty minutes, the trail ended where the narrow gorge opened into a massive valley. While I could no longer see the falls, the sandstone cliffs and dense vegetation of the Kangaroo Valley stretched out before me.

It was a breathtaking site and Michael gave me a few minutes to soak in the view before saying, *"Look back into the gorge, Little One."* I turned, and a few yards inside the entrance to the gorge, I saw the arc of the outside wall of the matrix. It was the color of living sunlight, filled with slivers of silver light darting in every direction as it created a dance of pure delight. The matrix was over 160 feet tall and more than a mile in diameter, which made it impossible for me to see from the falls!

Michael then had me return to the other side of the gorge and sit down on a bench near the falls. *"Relax and close your eyes, Little One. Take a few deep breaths, and ask to activate the matrix. Now open your eyes and visualize a rainbow coming out of your ascending heart chakra and simply let the rainbow flow into the falls where it chooses."*

Immediately, I felt a wave of energy flowing out of my chest and then split in two as it approached the waterfall. The first arc connected into the top of the right ribbon of water and the second entered just below the point in which the water joined into a single flow. There were two doorways!

As my rainbows reached out to the falls, Michael opened his side of the doorways and I saw the white light of the Angelic Realm appear before me. However, this time, the light didn't just flow into the open space of the cylinder; it flowed back along my rainbow and into my ascending heart. As the pure love of the Angelic Realm entered my physical being, tears of joy began to flow uncontrollably, and I became acutely aware of the fact that this place had just taken complete and total notice of me. It felt both strange and a little embarrassing to have all the animals, plants, rocks, water, and even the air looking at me.

Then suddenly, I felt Carrington Falls and the Kangaroo Valley reach out and pull me into the pure love of its consciousness. As I melted into the oneness of this magnificent place, I knew that this bond could never be broken. I had been searching all my life for the meaning of being both human and Spirit, yet suddenly and without warning, I had felt the true purpose of my human existence: ONENESS WITH MOTHER EARTH!

I stayed at the falls for most of the day, getting to know individual trees, bushes, flowers, rocks, and animals. Finally, it was time to go, and with a final prayer and overwhelming sense of gratitude, I walked away knowing that this place on Earth would draw me back to it over and over again, if not in person then in the twilight of my dreams.

The following day, I returned to Sydney and spent the day playing tourist. As I walked the crowded streets of downtown Sydney, I began to feel something I had never experienced before. I am a small town girl and even the energy of Colorado Springs often overwhelms me and causes me to be on constant alert. However, this sunny day I found myself reaching out to make eye contact with as many people as possible, and as I sat in the park at Dawes Point, I struck up conversations with dozens of people. I had never felt so safe and secure! That night in my hotel room, I asked Michael where this sudden burst of extroversion had come from.

"Little One, your new connection with Mother Earth woke up a part of you that has been hidden for many lifetimes. This awakening within you allows you to connect with all other humans who have made the same choice to awaken to the One Soul of Earth. Today you felt the desire and freedom to share your life with other humans like you, and there are a lot of humans choosing oneness in Australia. In fact, most of the people living in Australia have stepped into the Angelic Movement and are already consciously creating the new world of love.

"The creation of the new world is beginning on this continent and is flowing across the Pacific Basin as you will soon see in New Zealand. The connection between primal Earth and modern man has begun the creation of a new community of love and peace in which each life consciousness, regardless of form, will be honored and cared for.

"Enjoy, Little One, you are experiencing a piece of the new world!"

chapter thirty-two

Franz Josef Glacier

"Don't look back, Little One, just go with the flow." My plane had just taken off from Sydney and I was looking backwards from my window seat, desperately trying to hold onto the continent that I had fallen in love with.

I must admit that Michael's instructions brought a great relief to my aching neck, but as usual, I was pretty sure that Michael's words held more than one meaning. "Michael, is there something I need to know about the New Zealand matrix before we get there?"

"This matrix is even larger than Carrington Falls and it is essential that you approach it with an open heart and allow your energy to flow freely through all aspects of the ritual. Relax, have fun, and be in the moment!"

Several hours later, we flew over the southern island of New Zealand and landed in Christchurch. It took less than twenty minutes to cross the beaches, snow-covered mountains, and farmlands of New Zealand. The beauty of the land below me was almost more than my mind could comprehend. From Christchurch, we flew back over the island to the town of Hokitika.

The other eight passengers on the plane were from Hokitika and the surrounding area and gave me a quick lesson in how to speak New Zealand English. I loved the rhythms of the language, and my pronunciations seemed to impress many of the natives that I met over the next few days. Once in Hokitika, I rented a car and headed south.

Driving in New Zealand turned out to be problematic for me. While I was comfortable driving on the left side of the road and yielding at the narrow one-lane bridges, the beauty of the island around me was very distracting. As the snow covered Alps rose to great heights on my left, the deep blue Tasmanian Sea on my right incessantly called to me as it deposited foam and driftwood onto its wide sandy beaches. When I turned inland, I discovered miles of aqua blue lakes set within ancient grey and white rock formation, as well as green pastures, bright tropical plants, and dense forests created from a hundred different shades of green.

All of this beauty sat below a deep blue sky filled with white clouds that turned to pink as day gave way to dusk. I would drive for a few minutes and then have to stop along the side of the road to simply take in the view, say a prayer of gratitude, and cry for a few minutes. I was on sensory overload for the entire one hundred miles of the trip to Franz Josef.

There were only a few small towns in this area of New Zealand, so my trip allowed me to be alone with Michael for most of the drive. I will always treasure the silent closeness that we shared on this day, as the serenity and beauty of my Earthly world truly rivaled the beauty we shared in Michael's world. There were no words that could describe what I was feeling as the colors of this place simply melted into the colors of my soul.

I arrived in the town of Franz Josef and checked into my motel just as the first stars began appearing in the night sky. The following morning, I awoke refreshed and excited about visiting the Glacier. My first stop included checking in at the tour company and picking up instructions for the following day's tour, then grabbing a few snacks at the local grocery store before heading for the trail head of the glacier.

I had always associated snow, wind, dog sleds, and polar bears with glaciers, so getting out of the car in tennis shoes and a light jacket and walking along the well-manicured trail of the temperate rain forest was a pleasant sensation. Perhaps this matrix was not going to be as taxing on my body as I had expected.

Wrong again! As I exited the forest, I saw the glacier for the first time and wondered what Michael had gotten me into this time. The view was spectacular! This seven-and-a-half-mile-long glacier appeared deceptively small as it flowed downward between the massive green walls of two surrounding mountains. Even the mile-and-a-half rock covered river valley that stood between my position and the base of the glacier seemed to be a minor inconvenience.

A half hour later and still a long way from the glacier, I stopped for a breather and took a closer look at the rocks beneath me. Many of them were bluish grey and decorated with white swirling ribbons and a coating of sparkling silver. While they came in many shapes and sizes, I liked the round flat ones and decided to pick up a few on my way back. I used the larger rocks to cross the river without getting my feet wet and continued on. There were a lot of people in the valley and those I met returning from the glacier urged me on.

Just as I reached the base of the glacier, it began to rain. I got out my trusty umbrella and Michael directed me to the left side of the glacier where the river flowed into the valley through an opening beneath the ice. It took a little climbing to get to just the right spot and once there, I looked around to discover that all the other tourists had headed back down the trail.

I was the only person left at the glacier. The rain was coming down harder, and my mind immediately asked what all those people knew that I didn't know. I wasn't even sure if lightning was a problem on a glacier. *"Little One, you are fine. We just need privacy to set the matrix."*

I took out my crystal, and with the stick I had picked up in the rainforest, I opened each chakra, surrendered to the power and presence of God within me, and released the matrix to Michael. I felt a swoosh of energy and for a brief moment saw a ball of white energy leave my body and disappear into the rain and mist that was descending upon the glacier. Then Michael asked me to move to the right side of the glacier and repeat the process facing the opposite direction, and I felt more energy release from the center of my back.

I had no idea what we were doing, so I just went with the flow and after a few minutes felt really giddy and started laughing. I was glad no one was around because I knew they would have thought I was crazy. A few minutes later, as the rain began to let up, people began to return to the glacier and I headed back down the trail.

The following morning (October 9, 2009), I joined several hundred other people on a glacier tour. The sun was shining and the temperature was warm, but we were informed that there were gale force winds coming down the glacier. I was hoping the tour company had special permission to drive the tour busses right up to the base of the glacier, but no such luck. After walking against strong winds for over an hour, we put on our crampons and started up the side of the glacier. I chose to go in the final group and placed myself right behind the guide, which by the way is the position of the person least likely to complete a glacier walk.

Now for those of you who have never been on a glacier tour, let me explain that the guides cut steps into the steep sides of the glacier. The height of some of the steps fell just below my waist forcing me, at times, to pull myself up with my arms as I literally crawled up a wall of ice on my knees. In addition, as the sun shone down and the wind continued to blow, the steps began to melt. I must offer my utmost gratitude to the young tour guide who encouraged me all the way up the glacier on his first day on the job. I have often wondered if he chose to continue in this profession.

At one point, we walked through an ice cave where we stopped to rest and take pictures. The compressed ice of a glacier creates layers and ribbons of blue running through its white structure, but the inside of this cave was completely blue. It was the color of Michael, and as I instinctually reached out to touch him, the energy of the glacier rose to meet me and I felt its wisdom and agelessness.

I also felt something else that I can only describe as pure emotion. There was joy and sorrow, hope and despair, anger and forgiveness, peace and restlessness, contentment and emptiness, self-love and guilt, trust and anxiety, and so many more that I could not separate them in the moment. It was as if the sum of all of Mother Earth's past emotions lay frozen in the ice. The consciousness of this glacier and the emotions within me seemed to melt into oneness, and through this joining, I suddenly felt a complete and total love and acceptance for all the emotions of the Earth plane.

It was as if the glacier was a living vessel of love that had the ability to really experience, understand, and embrace the spiritual meaning and power of the emotions that run through our planet, yet I was confused by a voice deep inside the glacier echoing the phrase, *"Let her flow."*

As we left the ice cave, I felt a rush of energy flow through me and knew we were approaching the top of the glacier. One more set of steps and I found myself standing on the top of the glacier in the bright sunlight. The winds were tremendous and my tour guide informed me that we had to keep moving. We crossed the ice and were at the top of another set of steps when he asked me to wait there while he went back to get the rest of the group who had stopped to take pictures. I was alone on the ice and knew Michael had arranged this so we could open the doorway.

I turned to face the top of the glacier, took three deep breaths, and opened my heart to the glacier. I felt a rush of energy as a rainbow shot out the front of my ascending heart and split into three pieces. The first arc reached out to the top of the glacier, almost seven miles away, while the second and third arcs went to the left midsection of the glacier and right section of the glacier just above my position. Simultaneously, I felt another arc shoot out of my back and land on a section of the glacier below me. There were four doorways!

Instantly, the roar of the wind in my ears ceased and four strands of violet energy came up out of the glacier and rushed back along the arcs into my physical body. I would have fallen over if the energy entering my back from below had not helped balance the energy entering from above. This energy was immense in size yet so familiar to me that it filled me to the very depths of my being. Its softness and sweetness soothed me as it created a wholeness within me that allowed me to stand in the stillness of my soul. I suddenly felt my deepest longings disappear as my body, mind, and emotions reached out to hold onto this experience for just one moment.

In the silence of that moment, I heard a snap, like a stick breaking, and in my mind's eye saw a chopstick broken into two jagged pieces held precariously together by a single filament of bamboo. Suddenly the roar of the wind filled my ears and Michael's energy was wrapped tightly around me. *"Little One, we have to get you off the glacier safely. We need you to focus only on each physical step you take. Look at your feet and think of nothing else."*

I knew there was a problem. *"Little One, listen to me and concentrate on each step. Feel your body and think only about the step you are taking. Talk to me, Little One. Tell me what your body is doing!"*

The tour guide and the rest of the group had returned, and as we continued on our way, I began to focus on my feet. The descent took almost forty minutes and Michael kept bringing me back to my body whenever my mind would wander for even a fraction of a second. It was exhausting. I had never realized how many of my body movements were on automatic.

Once we arrived at the base of the glacier and took off our

crampons, Michael pulled back a little and I was able to relax my focus, drink some water, and eat a candy bar. I asked him what had happened and he told me we would talk about it later.

The walk back to the bus was easy; the gale force winds were now pushing us along. About halfway back, Michael asked me to stop, turn around, and close my eyes for a moment. When I opened them, I saw the outside curve of the matrix. The matrix walls were pure white with tiny violet flecks and I could see through them to the golden cast of the Angelic energy rushing upwards out of the four doorways in the ice. In the hour that the doorways had been open, the Angelic energy had filled the entire matrix and was beginning to pour over the tops of the surrounding mountains and into the valley below.

The glacier itself seemed to be alive, with hundreds of violet lightning bolts that rose from deep within the ice to merge into the four plumes of the Angelic Doorways. It was as if every inch of ice had taken on new life. I could feel the primal power of its softness and taste the sweetness of its core. I could not explain it, but I knew that my soul and this place were not just connected—they were one.

Within minutes, the matrix disappeared forever from my physical senses, but the sight of this Earthly glacier still had the power to bring peace into every atom of my being. I did not know what had happened to me, I only knew that the activation of this matrix was enough for me in this lifetime.

I ate, returned to the motel, and took a shower. As I brushed my hair, large chunks began to fall to the floor. I was horrified and demanded that Michael talk to me right now! *"Little One, during the activation of the doorway, you manifested the desire to hold the energy in your mind, body, and emotions for just a moment. This desire stopped the flow of the energy for a mere second, causing an overload of energy in your body that split a section of your DNA.*

"Since the damage occurred at the DNA level, it will take a few weeks for the symptoms to manifest in your physical body. The strands that were damaged affect your metabolism, blood chemistry,

and bone structure. That is why we needed to get you off the glacier safely. If you had broken a bone or injured yourself in any way, your body would have difficulty healing at this point.

"None of this damage is life threatening, but the healing will take many months and may be uncomfortable at times. Since you use your DNA to both create and activate the matrixes, we are unsure at this moment whether your body will be able to continue the matrix work in this lifetime."

Surprisingly, this information did not alarm me. I had known the risks before leaving the states, and my only reaction was to wonder how natural I would look in a wig. I went to bed feeling more peaceful than I could ever remember feeling.

Five hours later, I was awakened by a jolt that lifted me up off the bed and I immediately knew we were having an earthquake. However, that was it—just one jolt. I asked Michael what was going on and he said, *"We are connecting the Franz Josef doorway to the Carrington Falls doorway. What you are feeling is the rise of the energy from the glacier. Go back to sleep."* So I did.

The following day, I slowly drove back to Hokitika and then left for home on Sunday. The airline computers were down all day and flights were backed up at every airport. Yet the people of New Zealand were kind, gentle, and considerate amidst the chaos. One airport official told me, "We don't like to make a fuss." It was fun and refreshing to be around these independent people who had discovered the secret of expressing love even in the worst of situations. Spending time in their beautiful land helped me remember a kindness and gentleness within myself that I thought I had lost forever.

As my plane took off from Auckland, I felt a strange pull to the north that made me dizzy and a little nauseated. *"Little One, disconnect from the matrixes. We are triangulating the Australian and New Zealand doorways with a doorway recently opened in Japan in an attempt to further stabilize the plates of the Pacific Basin. Your DNA is not able to adjust; you must step out of the energy."*

I did as Michael asked and immediately felt better. "Have we done enough, Michael?"

"We don't know, but we have done all that we can do for now. Thank you for your help."

I ate dinner and then stretched out for the night. Due to the computer problems in New Zealand, very few people had made their connections and I had three seats all to myself. As I cuddled up with my pillow and blanket, I felt Michael wrap his energy around me with a softness and tenderness we had never before shared on Earth. Then he quietly asked, *"Little One, do you have any regrets?"*

I was absolutely sure about my answer. "No, Michael. If I had only one gift to give in this lifetime, it would be these doorways. I can't explain it, Michael, but I feel complete and totally happy for the first time in my life."

"Little One, the violet energy emanating from within the glacier is your own purple soul."

chapter thirty-three

HeartSong

I arrived home in Colorado an hour before I left New Zealand. Time is such a funny thing! I had waited forty-five years to bring Purple back into my body, and in one moment, released her back to the expression of love that she had so wisely chosen many years ago.

It was all very confusing for my mind, but I knew that this vibrant soft energy was still a part of me and that all the knowledge of her current existence was now available to me. Then two weeks after my return to the states, my physical body began to manifest some very unpleasant symptoms. Michael asked me to enter the matrix at Agnes Vaille Falls so the Angels could work on my body.

Buddy and I arrived at the falls on a warm sunny day in November. The leaves were gone and the canyon looked rather bare as it prepared for the upcoming winter. Michael had me spend about twenty minutes at the falls and then move down the canyon, stopping at each point where the energies of Melincourt, Cataratas, and Molasses Reef doorways were most concentrated.

Then he directed me to a large flat rock further down the

trail. *"Little One, we have not been able to fully integrate the new matrixes into your physical being due to the problem on the glacier. Your body heals from the inside out, so we are working from the first matrix outward in order to make the adjustments needed to allow the new energies to harmoniously flow through your body. We will need about thirty minutes, and Purple is waiting for you in Sacred Space to begin the healing of your mental and emotional patterns."*

Buddy was off chasing squirrels and chipmunks so I lay down, closed my eyes, and immediately found myself in my beloved valley. Pink Lady greeted me, and I noticed Green Guy, Orange, Yellow, and White attending to their chores in various parts of the valley as Blue stood upon his favorite mountaintop. As I started towards the opening of Purple's cave, Pink Lady informed me she was not there and pointed me in the direction of a new lake.

As I approached the edge of the water, I realized it was frozen and Purple was ice skating. I had not ice skated since I was a kid, so I sat down on the bank and waited for her to make the first move. Purple had always hid from me in the past, so I was pleasantly surprised when she raced over and sat down beside me.

Purple was the smallest member of my crew, but she was by far the most animated and energetic. She spoke very rapidly, shifting from one topic to another as if she could not keep up with her own curiosity, and her words were constantly interrupted by her loud laughter. Her purple silk dress was embroidered with shimmering silver butterflies, and fluttered around her knees as she excitedly pointed out the fur on the top of her skates. A headband made of white irises pulled her long violet hair away from her lilac face, revealing the depth of her deep green eyes, and upon her wrists she wore bracelets of multi-colored stones.

Even with the coordination of a child, Purple appeared totally confident in all her movements and a joyful Earthy innocence oozed out of every pore of her body. Purple held the wisdom and knowledge of the natural world and understood the trials of being a child on Earth, but she seemed to hold no understanding of the adult world of humans. Her perspective was fresh, fun, and magical as she caught me up on all of Pal and Happy's adventures. It seems that my Unicorn and Pegasus were still very much a part of her existence even if I had left them behind.

After rekindling the joy of my childhood, Purple became very serious. *"You were really mad when I left and I'm soooo glad you aren't mad at me anymore. I know you think I've been lost and confused, but I really do know who we are and why we are here. I have learned about things on my own and have to tell you that when we were little, I taught you some things that you now have to let go of.*

"When we were together, the physical world was new to us. The kidney defect in our body was unexpected and we did not know that the kidney problem and our physical pain were connected. We never knew when the pain would strike, so I taught you how to live in the future. Whenever the pain became too hard to bear, I took you out of time and let your human mind dream of a future without pain. I stayed with you until I knew the pain would disappear, but after I left, you kept living in the future.

"You have used the future to escape mental and emotional pain as well as physical pain. The problem is that in order to avoid pain, you also have to avoid love. Love can only be experienced in the moment, and I took that ability away from you. Do you understand?"

"I'm beginning to. I have missed you so much, and all these years, I truly have believed that my joy and ability to love and be loved left with you. I felt so guilty about losing you that I didn't realize that the love I so craved was still inside of me. When I felt you on the glacier, I knew deep inside of me who you were, and I just wanted to hold you inside of me for one more moment. I didn't realize how much you have grown."

"I am really big!"

"So what do we do now?"

"We are still a part of each other, like you and Blue. We just express in different ways in different places, but we can enter oneness when you are totally present in the moment, and you can always find me here in Sacred Space where there is no time. Let's play!" As I watched Purple slide across the ice, I could not help thinking that I must have been an interesting child.

I was pulled out of Sacred Space by cool wet Buddy kisses. My body felt warm, soft, and content. I thanked Michael, Rafael, and the entire Angelic Realm for their assistance as we started down the trail. Just above the entrance to the trailhead, I took a step that stopped me in my tracks. I immediately stepped backwards and felt the softness of the Franz Josef matrix.

The energy was so soft and subtle that I hadn't noticed it when I first entered it on my way up the trail. However, when I stepped out of the energy, the shift felt very dramatic. I thought about all the times that Michael had said, *"To know what love is, one must know what love is not."* It was only after I separated from the loving energy of the glacier that I was able to fully recognize and experience its love.

In the following weeks leading up the winter solstice, Michael continued to guide me through the first stages of healing my physical body. *"Little One, it is only possible to heal your mind, body, and emotions when you are experiencing them in the moment, so you must give up the future as well as the past. We promise you that you will be able to easily handle each moment of your healing, but if you try to project yourself into the future to see when and what is going to happen, you will miss taking the steps needed to complete this process.*

"The energy of the winter solstice of 2009 is adding the Angelic vibratory frequencies that most closely match the physical body, and this new energy will allow you to manifest your healing ten

times faster than you could have even a few months ago. We will know by the end of 2010 what your physical capabilities will be regarding the building of new matrixes. Let go of the outcome and what your future will be, and simply relax into your healing."

I wanted to give up my future, but quite honestly, I didn't know how. I had lived my whole life in the future, even reading and interpreting the creative energy that flowed outward to the world in order to predict what experiences would soon be appearing before me.

"Little One, the future was created out of a need for protection. Humans have many conscious and unconscious fears. Should you begin to manifest all your fears instantaneously, it is likely that you would do so much harm to yourself and the planet that your lifespan would be reduced to a few seconds at most. Slowing down energy creates the past, present, and future as a safety valve or safe period of time in which to review and make conscious choices about what you truly desired to manifest and experience on the Earth plane.

"You do not need to be protected from love, joy, and bliss, so as you move into your new energy and allow Spirit to create only loving experiences, the future becomes less and less necessary. In fact, speeding up the manifestation on your planet will eventually totally wipe out the future. Any thought, emotion, or desire that you have will instantaneously manifest, so if you are wondering what will happen in the future, it will automatically happen in the moment.

"We do not want to alarm you; instantaneous manifestation across the planet is still many generations away. However, each life consciousness is now physically manifesting both love and fear three to ten times faster than last year, and this speed of creation will continue to dramatically increase over the next few years."

This information made perfect sense to my mind and felt intuitively correct, but it still didn't tell me how to release the future. *"When you are totally and completely embracing your*

HeartSong, there is no need or desire to live in or even think about the future."

"What's a HeartSong?"

"It is the Angelic energy that you have chosen to BE in your new world of love. From an Angelic point of view, it is a specific vibratory frequency, but in human terms, it is the gift that you most want to create on the Earth plane. Little One, your HeartSong is peace. You are the energy of peace, and by simply holding this energy within your physical being, everything you think, feel, say, and do creates peace in your world."

I had a huge knee-jerk reaction to these words. "Michael, my energy can't be peace! I have done nothing but fight for what I have wanted and needed my whole life. I have experienced nothing but power struggles and conflicts in most of my relationships, jobs, education, and attempts to make enough money just to survive. Even my physical being and Spirit often seem to be at odds with one another."

"Little One, to know what peace is—one must know what peace is not. Struggle comes from trying to be that which you can never be. It's time to stop fighting and simply allow yourself to BE who you are. It's time to let go of the belief that you must make things right for Purple, and trust that Purple is and has always been exactly where she needs and desires to be.

"Walk away from fear by offering yourself peace of mind, embracing the serenity of loving all your emotions, and treating your body with honor, respect, and gentleness as it heals. Release the need to do something in order to create what you want, and know that the energy of peace within you creates everything you need and desire in this world. Sing a song of soft words and take gentle actions, and all those you touch will hear your words and both know and love who you are."

I had learned through my experience on the glacier that my struggle to hold on to the past and try to control the future merely served to split my physical being. As I gently and softly reached out to embrace a new way of living in my heart, I heard the childlike voice of Purple begin to sing my favorite childhood Christmas Carol:

> "Let there be peace on Earth,
> And let it begin with me.

> Let there be peace of Earth,
> The peace that was meant to be…"

Purple was right—children really do know who they are and why they are here!

chapter thirty-four

Write The Book

"Little One, you do not need to learn how to love, you need to learn how to express love." I had been hearing those words from Emmanuel and Archangel Michael for over fifteen years, and yet this phrase still seemed as elusive as ever.

As my world moved into 2010, I knew that I wanted to live in a world of peace. As I sat in the bubble of my own energy, I could feel the vibration of peace within me, hear its song in my heart, see its color within my mind, taste its sweetness, and even smell its energetic fragrance. Peace filled me to overflowing, but I still had no idea how to express this love to a culture that seemed to be totally focused on supporting fear's last stand.

Everywhere I looked, I saw war, abuse, hurtful relationships, polarization, and people struggling to hold onto the illusions of their standard of living and rigid belief systems. I felt isolated and alone in my desire to live in peace with others, and longed for the sense of oneness and tribal belonging that I had experienced in Wales and Australia.

"Little One, if it becomes too painful for you to continue living in the United States, we will help you move to an area where you can

experience living with a soul group. However, your heart still belongs with Buddy and your father, and the energy of Pikes Peak supports your physical healing at this time. Your energy is also greatly needed in your country, and we want to assure you that by placing yourself in an environment where fear is valued over love, you will be able to recognize the differences between fear and love more easily.

"This discernment will allow you to increase the rate at which you learn how to express love over the next few years, further integrating your Spirit and humanity into oneness. From your Spirit's point of view, you are in the most loving place possible for you in this moment, but know that Spirit will never let you suffer. When it becomes more loving for you to move across your planet or even come home to us, it will happen almost instantly!"

Michael's statement that Spirit would never let me suffer seemed to be radically tested in the first few months of 2010. I had not been sick or seriously injured in the last five years; even my trek through the jungles of Peru had not produced more than a blister on my foot and a few days of exhaustion. Now it seemed as though each day brought new pain and discomfort into my body. Sore throats, sinus infections, the flu, and colds were common occurrences, and I could not keep my body temperature above ninety-five degrees, which left me feeling cold all the time. I was eating very little yet gaining weight and could literally feel my metabolism shutting down.

In February, I woke up with a pain in my left knee, which I had injured years before, and it took me a month and a half to heal it. I was anemic and my bones, joints, and muscles ached all the time. By mid-March, I had decided that my body was completely falling apart due to aging and my life needed to come to a merciful end!

In addition to my body, the rest of my life was slipping away as well. I was unable to open a temporary matrix for others due to the injury at Franz Josef, and I placed all my classes and energy work on hold. The radio station moved to a new location in January and my show came to an end. My phone readings actually increased during this period, allowing my income to remain steady, but my physical contact with people and the outside world dramatically decreased.

Buddy was my constant companion and the only thing that kept me going during this time. He kept the magic flowing into our lives as he patiently sat by my side on days when I lacked the energy to do anything but feed him and let him out for quick potty breaks.

Then one day in late March, I woke up, took a bath, got dressed, and let Buddy out before I even noticed that my body was free of pain. In fact, it felt incredibly strong, warm, soft, clean, and completely relaxed. The more I tuned into my body, the happier and more content I became. It was as if the war within my body had ended and the joy of peace finally flowed freely through my being once again.

I was almost afraid to ask if this change was permanent or merely a short reprieve, when Michael assured me, *"The healing of your DNA is complete and while your body will continue to heal all old injuries and dormant illnesses in your body, this process will result in only minor irritations from this point on. You still have some healing of your lungs, jaw, and kidneys and may attract a sinus infection or cold in the future, but you will be able to easily handle any symptoms. In fact, your body is healthier and stronger right now than at any previous time in your life.*

"Little One, we must also tell you that your DNA did not heal as we had hoped. The tear in your DNA healed with a slight ridge running down its center, much like your keloid kidney scar. While this will not affect the functioning of your body, it will affect your ability to create new matrixes. If you attempt to pull the energy through these DNA strands, the extra thickness of the ridge will prevent the energy from flowing through at the same rate as the surrounding area, leaving a hole or weak spot in the matrix wall. This weakness will cause the wall to fail as the Angelic energy enters the Earth plane.

"We are still looking at other ways in which you might create future matrixes, but at the present time your body does not have the

capability to continue this piece of your path and it is unsure whether it ever will. You will still be able to open and work with the completed matrixes as before and there is much more to your path than opening Angelic Doorways. Little One, do you have any regrets?"

"No, Michael. I am sad and disappointed and I feel like I have lost a part of myself, but I have no regrets. If I had it to do all over again knowing what I now know, I would do it without hesitation. I know that trying to hold Purple in my body caused this problem, but we are in oneness now and I am totally fulfilled. My gratitude for this gift greatly overwhelms my sadness and disappointment."

As my health continued to improve and my energy began to increase, I found myself with time on my hands. Gone were my afternoon naps and daily preparations for the radio show, and my readings, while increasing, did not take up all of my days. Then one day, I was sitting at the computer toying with the idea of teaching a summer seminar when I typed the sentence, "Recently, I have chosen an Angel as my life partner."

I cringed even before Michael said, *"Write the book!"* I had written a Master's Thesis in the '70s and found the process both grueling and unsatisfying. As I began teaching classes, many of my students suggested I write a book about Michael. However, each one of them wanted me to discuss a different topic in detail and I just couldn't get excited about any of them.

I have known many individuals who seem to feel an overwhelming need to write, and I stand in awe of all those that are driven to fill a blank piece of paper with their worlds, but I am not one of those people. So I asked Michael, "Why in the world would I write a book?"

"It's time, Little One. Do you remember how you felt when you read your Great Great Grandfather Galloway's book?"

"I loved that book!"

"Why do you love it? The writing is very straightforward, unemotional, and dry. It is a memoir of a life written by a man with very little education."

"It's not the writing; it's the story. Here is a man who lived in the community where I grew up and fought in the Civil War. When I read the book, I feel a direct connection to pioneer life in Illinois and the war that forced us to deal with the darkness of slavery. The history books glorify the fighting, but Grandpa's book gives a simple picture of the pain and devastation it inflicted on everyone involved. It felt real to me."

"The Civil War was a turning point in the history of not only your country, but the planet. It resulted in a huge increase in the vibratory frequency of the United States that was felt around the world. It was a step in Earth's movement into the new paradigm. Joseph's book was created for his children and the generations of his family to come so that the knowledge and memories would live on. Your world can never give up the wisdom learned in the past or you will be forced to repeat the lessons that created it.

"You are not evolving into something new, you are expanding into more of what you are. The Angelic Movement is the greatest turning point Earth has ever known. Five generations from now, your ancestors will read the book you leave behind and marvel at the struggle you went through to bring the Angelic energy to Earth. Allow your story of partnering with an Angel to be simply stated."

I could feel my heart and mind opening to the idea of writing my love story with Michael, but there was still the problem of actually sitting down and writing it. *"Little One, this process will be different from the writings of your past because you and your world are different. Your isolation of the past few months has allowed you to disconnect from the fear-based Collective Consciousness of Man and plug into the universal knowledge of the Angelic Realm."*

I suddenly understood why I had lost all interest in television, movies, and world events over the last few months. I had to admit that pulling out of the fear-based world had created a soft, peaceful life for Buddy and me, but I was still confused on how that would help me write a book.

"During the last winter solstice (2009), the One Soul of Earth made the decision to pull additional vibratory frequencies into the Earth plane, in essence adding all the energies that were planned between now and 2013."

"Does this mean that the energy of 2012 has already arrived?"

"Yes, and it has brought with it some unexpected side effects."

"Do I want to know about this, Michael?"

"Probably not, but we're going to pull you into the spiritual loop anyway. The energy of 2012 split the planet. Individuals must now choose which energy to use and you have chosen love, which means you can only deal with others who have also chosen love. This is why your radio show ended and why you can no longer do readings for some of those who approach you. You have chosen to hold the light of peace and anyone who is not ready to seek peace can no longer hear your messages.

"The split in energy on the planet has also pushed many life consciousnesses that were moving back and forth between the fear- and loved-based energies into the Angelic Movement. With more individuals expressing love, the energy waves on your planet have increased in size and number, with a new wave being created every two weeks. Unique pieces of universal knowledge are contained in each wave, and the moment you disconnected from the Collective Consciousness, you gained access to all the Angelic information within them.

"Little One, by plugging into universal knowledge from both within your own experience and from the world around you, you can write this book with the knowledge, wisdom, and perceptions of both your Spirit and human mind." I had no clue how to do this. *"You will create the book the way you have created your matrixes."*

Now that I understood, I would simply have to listen and see what appeared before me and then offer it to the world. *"Yes, Little One, the book is not information channeled from one realm to another, it is simply the story of the past fifteen years of your life as experienced by both your humanity and your Spirit.*

"The paradigm shift is the hardest thing any human being has ever undertaken. There is much confusion in trying to create something completely new in the midst of the memory of your past. Writing the book will allow you to see where you have been through the loving perceptions of your Spirit. Only by loving your past can you truly make peace with it. Write the book, Little One, and you will discover that the story of your life is an expression of love!"

chapter thirty-five

The Power Of Love

Who knew that while the human Viki was struggling through life, the Spirit within was having so much fun? Now I am not saying that Spirit wants humans to suffer or enjoys the suffering of humans; in fact, I am absolutely sure it does not. I am simply saying that while the human Viki was focused almost entirely on the fear and negativity of life, Spirit was focused on the love and joy.

As I listened to Spirit tell the story of my life and then chimed in with my own human view, my story began to expand before my eyes. I never knew what was going to show up on the page in front of me, and I was continually surprised at the moments and experiences that Spirit chose to share. Only as the chapters began to unfold did the threads of my hidden Divine Plan begin to emerge.

I was not experiencing simple memories or hindsight; it all felt as if it was happening in this moment. It was fun, highly emotional, often cathartic, and always surprising. Somehow through the process of writing the book, I began to fall in love with my life. I began to realize that the struggles and pain in my life had forced me to seek the unknown within, and that this journey had brought a happiness and joy into my life that was sweeter than anything my human mind alone could have ever imagined.

As spring turned into summer, Buddy and I experienced a joy and peace in our lives that we had never known before. I slowed down and really looked at the beauty in the world around me as Buddy stopped to smell the roses, grass, dog poop, and anything else he could find. I found myself grateful for every little thing in my life and began to seek out only positive loving people and experiences. It did not take long for the majority of the negative aspects of my life to fall away, and all the pain that remained quickly showed its loving purpose in my life.

Then just when I thought things couldn't get any better, Michael said, *"Little One, why don't you trust me to take care of you financially?"* I felt like I had just been shot with a stun gun! I had never even considered the possibility of being financially supported by Michael. Over the last fifteen years, I had done hundreds of readings with Michael in which our clients were offered many opportunities to increase their wealth, but never once had I heard Michael tell someone to quit their job and then offer to financially support them. "Are you capable of supporting me, Michael?"

Immediately, Michael pulled me into the Angelic Realm and I melted into its infinite oneness. Michael asked me to focus on the energy of the physical realm, and a moment later, I was back in my body hearing Michael ask, *"Which realm has more energy?"* I got the point. *"Now why don't you trust me to take care of you financially?"*

"You never offered. Are you offering to take care of me financially?"

"Are you asking?"

"Yes."

"Then I am offering. Little One, it is time for you to take the next step towards fulfillment, and that requires that you live in financial abundance. Fear has taught you that no one else will care for you and

if you do not work, you will find yourself homeless and hungry. For the majority of your life, you have done what others have expected of you in order to make money and support yourself. Most of this work was in direct conflict with your heart's desire and your spiritual beliefs, and because of this, you have become uncomfortable with money.

"You currently believe that Spirit does not understand the concept of money on your planet, but we want to assure you that we understand the material needs of your planet very well. However, we cannot intrude upon your beliefs and emotions surrounding money, so we asked you to release them and allow us to fully support you on Earth."

I wanted nothing more than to let go of my money issues, but I still believed in the Law of Attraction and the need to focus on what I wanted, and felt skeptical about giving up control over my finances. *"Little One, we are not asking you to give up the Law of Attraction, we are asking you to expand into the Law of Creation."*

"What's the difference, Michael?"

"The Law of Attraction allows you to attract any energy that is currently on the Earth. You can attract something that is already in physical form or you can utilize energy that is currently undergoing transformation on the planet to customize your creation, but the energy in the Law of Attraction always comes from the vibratory frequencies of the Earth plane. In other words, you are using energy currently being cycled through the original power plant and grid of the Earth. This method of manifestation often places you into competition for energy with all other life consciousness on the planet and can take a great deal of time, focus, and strength to pull in. Little One, at times you have felt that you must use force to complete this process and your aversion to force has caused you to pull away and ask for less than you need.

"The Law of Creation allows you to utilize your own body to pull the energy of the Angelic Realm into the Earth and create what you

want in your own energy field. This process literally adds energy of higher vibratory frequency to the planet, and since Angelic energy immediately begins to expand in the physical realm, an individual consciousness can create what they want and still have additional energy to pour into the new power plant and grid. There is no competition for energy; the more abundance an individual creates, the more it has to offer the planet.

"At the present time on Earth, most human minds are not able to manifest with Angelic energy; however, Spirit has the ability to easily create with this energy, and it knows both what is best for you and what your mind, body, and emotions desire. By surrendering to Spirit's manifestation through the Law of Creation, your abundance will grow in ways you cannot imagine."

I ached for a sense of financial freedom, but I had no idea of how to achieve it. *"Little One, surrender your finances to me and place all your focus on being of service to others by doing what you love. Let go of reaching out to the world for survival and embrace the Divine Truth that all abundance on Earth comes from the God source within you. Believe that joy, play, and fun create your abundance and allow all that Spirit has to offer to quickly and easily flow into your life.*

"You must also realign your free will with Divine Love, or at times, it will block your use of the Law of Creation. During the origins of humanity, the One Soul of Earth created free will as an opportunity for the life consciousness of the planet to choose fear, and even with this gift, it took thousands of years for life on Earth to truly accept and believe in fear. However, once humanity entered fully into this altered state, free will became a forceful tool which continues to support fear on your planet."

The idea of free will suddenly took on a new more malevolent meaning, "Can I give it back?"

"No, nor should you. Through the Angelic Movement, the use of free will is being transformed from the ability to choose fear to that of choosing between the infinite expressions of Divine Love available

to you on the Earth plane. No individual can possibly express all the love they are in any given lifetime, so free will is a valuable tool that can create a structure in which one can experience a sense of complete fulfillment in each life. Once you understand the power of love and transform the use of your free will, you will be able to create and express all your gifts on the Earth plane.

"*It will be painful, confusing, and frightening at times, but we urge you to allow yourself to open to the mysteries of your own creations and let your love flow into a world yet to be seen.*" I knew in my heart that Michael had always taken care of me, so I took a leap of faith and surrendered my finances to my life partner!

A few weeks later, on a warm afternoon in June, I was walking in the park with Buddy when I sat down under my favorite tree, and noticed that I felt a little off balance. I tuned into my body and discovered an empty sadness in my heart and stomach. Of course, my first thought was that I needed to eat some chocolate, but then I realized this feeling went much deeper.

During the previous four years, June had been the month in which I began thinking about my trip to open the next Angelic Doorway. However, when I reached inside, there was no new matrix, no trip to be planned, and no new adventure on the horizon. I knew that my sense of emptiness came from a human longing rather than a lack of spiritual fulfillment; my body, mind, and emotions had gotten use to the routine of building a matrix each year. Instinctively, I turned to my Sacred Space and soul essences to help me release my sadness and try and discover a new life's passion.

I checked on Buddy, who was chasing squirrels nearby, and then closed my eyes and took a few deep breaths. A few moments later, Buddy lay down next to me with his head and front paws in my lap—evidently Buddy wanted to go into Sacred Space with me. I took a few more deep breaths and found myself in the entrance of my sacred valley.

Pink Lady and Green Guy were there to greet me, Blue was on

the mountaintop, Purple was sailing on the lake, Orange was shooting flaming arrows into the sky, and Yellow and White appeared to be sharing a picnic nearby. Hoping for chocolate, I headed for the picnic with Pink Lady and Green Guy following close behind. I was about halfway there when I saw Buddy come loping across the valley with a figure on his back. As they neared, I realized that Buddy was carrying a Black Knight wearing full armor and carrying a sword. As they stopped before me, the Knight dismounted, and Buddy licked my face and then ran off across the valley.

As the Knight removed his helmet and armor, I was pulled towards him by a strong sense of recognition. I had no idea how I knew this soul essence or what his purpose in my Earthly life would be, but my emotional reaction was so intense that we immediately embraced and shared a rather passionate kiss. It would seem that I really do have a thing for spiritual beings that carry swords, and there was definitely something about this energy that awoke a deep sexual and creative energy deep within me. While there was no overt cheering or even a comment of any kind from the rest of the crew, they did seem to disappear into the valley rather quickly leaving us alone to get to know one another on our own terms.

My Knight's black skin and thick wavy hair glistened with silver fairy dust, and the dark brown of his irises surrounded the gold light emanating from his eyes. In contrast to the cold hardness of his armor, the robe he wore underneath was made of warm black suede. His large muscular body reflected great physical strength, yet when he reached out to me and opened his hand, safely cradled within were two hummingbirds. As he released them, they flew towards me gently caressing my cheeks and hair with their beating wings before flying off into the valley. He spoke with a voice so soft and gentle that it filled me with wonder.

"I am Black of Archangel Uriel, and I possess the creative power of the void and all that is yet to be. I am your provider and playmate, the writer and poet within you, and the next essence needed to

balance your male and female energy on the physical planet. I have served as a Spirit Guide and Guardian Angel to you since your birth on this planet, and I now ask to join you in the physical plane as an essence of your being for the remainder of this life. I bring you the joy of creativity and the universal knowledge of personal power and free will. Together we possess the strength to create the new world within your physical being and the courage needed to express those creations to the outer world."

I felt overwhelmed and confused in the presence of Black's soft power. I had always defined power as the ability to get what I wanted, and more often than not, this had required money or a display of some type of physical, mental, or emotional forcefulness on my part. Black possessed neither money nor force—his power was based in softness, gentleness, kindness, and peace. While my whole being ached to express this power, it seemed well beyond the reach of my human existence.

Black sensed my confusion and explained, *"True power is the flow and creation of Divine Love through your physical being. Love is the essence of who you are and by its very nature is soft, gentle, and expands you beyond the need and reach of force. The power of love lies in your willingness to receive all that you need and desire simply by allowing the Spirit within you to create what is most loving for you in each moment.*

"True power manifests as an expression of love without any expectation that it will be heard, accepted, validated, or heeded by those in your world. But know that the infinite consciousness of the Angelic Realm will hear, acknowledge, and manifest each expression of your love in the physical realm.

As I embraced the gentle power of Black, I found myself encircled by the light of Pink Lady, Green Guy, Orange, Yellow, White, Blue, and Purple and felt the perfect balance of my four male and four female essences begin to flow through me. I opened my heart and allowed myself to permanently remove the mental and emotional armor that I had been wearing for so many years, knowing that the life of love we were about to create required no further force or protection.

In total vulnerability, I stood before the soft power of my Black Knight, knowing that my true spiritual gifts and the life that Spirit wanted to create for me were still very much a mystery to me. I invited him into my physical being, and as we merged, my body felt the presence of a Divine Love that it had unknowingly been yearning for since my arrival on Earth.

Unlike the innocence of my childhood, the knowledge gained through my years of separation finally crystallized into the wisdom I needed to make the conscious choice to join my Spirit and physical being in the true power of love!

chapter thirty-six

Not All Dogs Go To Heaven

"Ms. Hart, the doctor found a growth on Buddy's leg during his pre-dental examination and he would like to take it off while he has Buddy under anesthesia." I had dropped Buddy off for his yearly dental cleaning an hour earlier, and since the vet had removed another benign tumor a few years ago, I agreed without hesitation. I had several clients that day and barely had time to get them out of my office before it was time to pick up my dog.

The moment I stepped up to the receptionist's desk, she said, "I'm so sorry, the doctor is sure it's cancer." My whole body went numb and I couldn't seem to put two words together. The doctor did not want to speculate on a diagnosis or prognosis until he received the lab results and told me he would call the following week. As I set up the appointment to have his stitches removed, Buddy vocally demanded his treat and greeted the UPS man at the front door. I may have been in shock, but it was business as usual for my furry friend.

The vet's instructions included no running, jumping, or stairs, so upon our arrival at home, Buddy ran up stairs, jumped up on the bed, and proceeded to take a nap. Still dazed, I sat down in my rocking chair, and fully expecting Michael to tell me the tumor was benign, asked him what was going on. *"Little One, your life is about to change dramatically in the next few months and Buddy has other things to do, so he is leaving the Earth plane."* I felt my mind and emotions detach from this statement and decided that I would just wait for Dr. Regnier to call and straighten out this confusion.

The following Tuesday, the vet called and informed me that Buddy had a very rare form of cancer of the nerve endings. He had only seen five cases of this type of cancer in over twenty years of practice, but all seemed to follow a similar pattern. This cancer was very aggressive and usually metastasized very quickly. Unfortunately, the tumor had invaded the bone and surrounding tissues, and he had only been able to remove about seventy-five percent of the mass. Dr. Regnier explained that chemotherapy and removing the leg might extend his life, but there was no cure. He estimated that without treatment, Buddy would survive another two months.

No human had ever been able to figure out Buddy's breeding, but everyone agreed that this dog was created to run. Losing a leg would have changed who Buddy was, and that was not something I could consider. I also intuitively knew that the changes I had seen in Buddy over the last few months were not due to aging or arthritis—there were other tumors.

I went into Sacred Space with Buddy and asked him what he wanted, and he simply said, "I love you. I came to Earth to teach you how to love this physical world and I have done that. It's time for you to go out and express that love to the world and you won't do that if I stay." I cried for several hours and then called the vet and told him I wanted to make Buddy comfortable and let the cancer take its course. Dr. Regnier gently told me he would euthanize Buddy whenever I was ready.

The next month was soft and joyous. We spent most of our time softly playing and cuddling—my fifty-pound friend still thought he was a lap dog. Buddy tried to run a few times, but even after the incision healed, the leg was too weak to support an all out-effort.

When he began to show weakness in his back legs, we shortened our walks, and eventually drove to the park to spend a few minutes each day.

I was terrified that I would make the decision to put him down too soon or would wait too long, and one night I even had a vivid dream of being in a room with Buddy during his final minutes, but then dismissed it upon waking because I had never seen this room before. Michael just kept telling me to stay in the moment and listen.

Then on the Saturday before Labor Day, Buddy began crying and it was obvious he was in pain. I doubled up on his pain medication, which seemed to help, but he could not sit down and was having trouble moving his back left leg. I could feel him reaching out to my mind, trying to tell me something, but I wouldn't listen. I went upstairs, knowing he couldn't follow me.

When I reached the top of the stairs, I realized that he had already pulled all of his energy out of the upper floor of our home and quietly said, "Michael, I can't do this, not yet, we were supposed to have two months," and without thinking changed clothes and went back downstairs. Buddy was in the kitchen and when I approached him, I felt a sharp pain slice through my chest as he severed our heart connection. Stunned and sobbing uncontrollably, I heard Michael say, *"Little One, he is asking for your help, but if it's too hard, you do not have to do this now."* I wasn't ready, but I knew I would never be ready, so I called the weekend animal emergency clinic and informed them we were on our way.

The staff was kind and patient as they escorted us to the room I had seen in my dream, and a half hour later, Buddy gently licked my face and then turned to the vet as she administered the anesthetic. Just before the final injection was given, I felt Michael wrap his energy around me and saw Uriel move towards Buddy from the opposite side of the room. The vet listened for a heartbeat and then said, "He's gone. Take as much time as you need."

As she left the room, I reached out for the familiar warmth of the Angelic Realm but could not feel it. I don't know how long I stayed there touching his body and crying before I realized he had not left. His energy was so strong in that room that I got up to tell the vet that he was still alive, but when I stepped into the hallway his energy was still beside me. I asked Michael what was wrong and he said, *"Nothing is wrong, Little One. Buddy is okay and you need to go home."*

I thanked the staff and as I slid into the driver's seat, I was overcome with a deep sense of peace and serenity. As I drove home Michael explained, *"Buddy did not go into the Angelic Realm. While you were waiting for the doorway to the Angelic Realm to open, Buddy slipped through the veil between your world and the fairy world. The Fairy Realm lies between the Earth and Angelic Realm in density and that is why you can feel him so intensely. Uriel accompanied him through his transition and Buddy is exactly where he needs and wants to be."*

This information scared me. I understood the joy and eternal love of the Angelic Realm, but my precious friend was in a world of which I had no experience or knowledge. Is there hunger, cold, illness, and suffering in the Fairy Realm? Would he be loved and taken care of? Why had he chosen this path?

The following day, I went to Celebration and my friend Heather Snowmoon, a Gypsy High Priestess and teacher of Fairy Wicca, helped me access the Tree Fairy who brought Buddy to me. I asked Buddy if he was all right and why he had gone into the Fairy Realm instead of the Angelic Realm and he simply said, *"In the Angelic Realm, you fly, but in the Fairy Realm, you run. I want to run."* Buddy was all right!

I was not. Michael had been explaining grieving with reverence to me since my mother died fifteen years earlier, but I knew that I had never really let myself feel this process. The day after Buddy died, I made a conscious choice to fully experience the depth of my grief, and for the first week, I cried continuously, sometimes sobbing so hard I could not take a breath and at other times simply letting hundreds of tears flow silently down my cheeks. I woke up crying, went to sleep crying, and even discovered how to eat while crying. The pain in the center of my chest was so intense that I believed I was about to die of a broken heart.

Through it all Michael was there, wrapping his soft energy around me. He told me when to eat, when to go to bed, when to take a bath. When the pain within my body became so intense that I could no longer bear it, he told me to groan. There is an instinctive groan that resonates so deeply from within our being that it literally has the power to dissolve physical, mental, and emotional pain. As a Doula, I had coached women in the use of this groan during childbirth, but Michael was now showing me how to use this inner power to deal with the physical pain of grief.

He also continually asked me to release all grief that did not belong in this moment to him, and as he began to take my grief over my mother, grandparents, aunts and uncles, cousins and friends, the pain became more bearable. In fact, at one point, I suddenly realized that the depth of my pain was a true reflection of the depth of the love that I had felt for Buddy. I was both surprised and shocked at this revelation; I had never known I was capable of loving this deeply on the Earth plane. There were even moments when I craved entering those depths, knowing that the experience of this pain honored all that my four-legged friend had been in this world.

A few days after Buddy died, Michael told me that the physical pain in my chest would subside in another five or six days. *"When someone dies, those left behind feel a hole within their physical bodies. While many people experience this hole as the loss of the energy of the individual who has died, it is really a hole within their own energy field. Humans often create specific expressions of love for each life consciousness in their lives. Over time, these expressions lead to the creation of a specific flow of energy from one person to another. For example, you opened your heart fully to Buddy so the energy flow came from the heart area.*

"When you open your mind to someone, the flow may emanate from the face and head while those you physically relate to may receive a flow from your hands, arms, torso, legs, or even feet. When someone you love dies, that energy flow is stopped and a hole appears. Part of the grieving process requires that you fill in that hole by allowing your spiritual energy to flow to another source. You may wisely use this energy to heal and fulfill your own needs or it may be redirected to someone else."

During the next week, I began asking to help someone else each day and found that at least during the time that I was doing a reading or completing some type of service for someone else, I was able to step outside of my own pain for a few hours. However, these brief reprieves came with a very painful side effect. In those first few weeks, I was stunned, time and time again, by how quickly I could forget that Buddy was gone.

Dogs are wonderful creatures that live in the moment and celebrate everything. Buddy was always waiting to celebrate my arrival home, my emergence from the bathroom, walks, eating, people walking down the street, squirrels racing in the trees, going to bed, getting up, dancing, tug of war, answering the phone, hanging up the phone, putting on shoes, talking to neighbors, garbage trucks, and everything else that life on Earth has to offer! My precious friend was the instigator of many dances of joy in our home.

In the weeks following his death, I automatically turned, time and time again, to share a dance with Buddy, only to be greeted with silence and the rush of grief that accompanied the remembering of his passing. The silence of the house was both deafening and comforting. Buddy had always been a very loud creature; he talked all the time and sounded like a horse when he walked. The silence of the house helped me remember he was gone and for the first few weeks, I did not turn on the television or stereo even once.

Those days also brought an overload of firsts: the first time I went to the mailbox without him, the first time I came home and he was not waiting at the door, the first time I ate a meal alone, slept alone, got up alone, answered the door alone, took a walk by myself, channeled a reading, and wrote a chapter without him at my side.

My crying shifted from constant to sporadic after the first seven days or so. Michael had been right, the physical pain did begin to subside and I actually thought I was functioning rather well. I had moved my bed, rearranged the furniture in my living room, and created a new daily routine. Still, I had the overpowering need and desire to take care of Buddy. Finally, after a month, I asked Heather Snowmoon to help me connect with Buddy in the Fairly Realm, and she taught me how to attune myself to his new world.

I went to the park, sat down under my favorite tree, closed my eyes, and asked Michael to help me with the attunement. Instantly, I sensed a shift in the tree behind me and the grass beneath me. Then I felt my beloved friend sitting next to me and opened my eyes. The world looked wavy, as if everything were covered with a soft flowing energy. I could not see Buddy with my eyes, but I could feel him and hear his flow of consciousness. I could also feel his happiness as he asked me to walk with him. At first, it was a little difficult for me to walk in all that wavy energy, but I soon became accustomed to its lightness.

As he began to talk about his current existence, I realized that Buddy was different. He was now totally free and unencumbered by the physical rules of my world. Buddy could not only run in the Fairy Realm, he could instantly move across the planet with a single thought. Buddy had been very upset when he could not go to Wales with me in 2007, and he was quick to tell me that he had visited Melincourt Falls and described its current condition and the fairies that served it in great detail.

There was more than just a change in physical form. Buddy had a very strong sense of purpose in his current life. He explained that he was a healer and served the Earth by bringing energy to the trees, plants, and animals. It was clear that Buddy was no longer attached to human consciousness; in fact, he didn't seem particularly interested in the human condition at all. Buddy was no longer a domesticated creature; he was wild. He reminded me of the wolf puppies I had encountered on one of my radio shows. The pups were aware of the humans around them, but couldn't care less about pleasing them. Buddy was no longer my dog, and while our spiritual connection was as strong as ever, he no longer needed or wanted me to take care of him.

We walked for a few minutes before I was able to face my greatest fear and ask Buddy if he was mad at me for having him put to sleep. He answered very matter-of-factly, *"I asked you to help me die and you did. I had two more tumors that were growing very rapidly, one on my back leg that was very painful and another in my spinal cord. In two more days, I would not have been able to walk, and I did not want to experience that."* While this statement served to ease my guilt, it also forced me to acknowledge how little I understood about my place in the Divine Plan.

I left the park with a new sense of peace and freedom. The last twelve years of my life had revolved around what I thought was best for Buddy and me. I had not considered moving anywhere Buddy could not go, and limited my work and the length of my trips to the amount of time that was comfortable to be away from him. Now just as Buddy could move freely around the planet, so could I, and just as Buddy had discovered who he was without me, it was time for me to discover who I was without him.

Before his death, Buddy told me it was time to for me to go out and express my love to the world. That had always been so easy for Bud and so hard for me. I could not help wondering if this wonderful Spirit had known when he left that I would use the gigantic hole he left behind to express my love in a new way, in a way that he had spent so many years trying to teach me.

Unfortunately, my new sense of peace was soon interrupted. Grief is irrational and mysterious; just when you think you have successfully navigated your way out of its clutches, it pulls you right back in with the slightest sound, sight, or memory. The trauma we incur through the death of another occurs in the time and place of their spiritual transformation, not ours, and so we are left to deal with our pain in a future that does not include them. However, I did know that Buddy would want me to dance in joy and continue to celebrate the moments we shared rather than regret those that will never be, and I also knew that I had the power within me to do so.

Over time, I began to realize that only by surrendering completely to my grief did I discover how much I truly love my friend. In the first few weeks of my grief, Michael told me never to say, "I loved Buddy," but to always say, "I love Buddy."

"Love never dies, Little One. It lives on in each moment of your eternal existence. Do not let yourself be separated from love by placing it in the past through your thoughts, feelings, actions, or statements."

Buddy taught me that the best loves of our lives challenge us, through both life and death, to continuously fill every speck of our being with the energy of spiritual love, and to use that love to create a rich new vibrancy of colors and songs for the world in which we live. We shared a life filled with Angels, oneness with Mother Earth, and touching universal knowledge and wisdom.

I had been so sure that I knew more about Angels and Divine Truth than most people on this planet, and then my best friend took me down a notch and forced me to open my heart and mind to yet another mystery of eternal life. Not all dogs go to Heaven; some of them go to the Fairy Realm!

chapter thirty-seven

One Final Question

I came out of the depths of my grief as more of me. When Buddy died, Michael created a safe place for me to dive into the darkness of my greatest fears and pain, and what I found hidden beneath all that blackness was my HeartSong.

I have always loved to listen to music at dusk. I let the music carry me along as the light of day slowly wanes and is replaced by soft blues, indigos, and finally a black sky filled with twinkling stars. I love how my eyes slowly adjust to the varying light, and as details turn into shadowy shapes, my mind begins to slow and finally comes to rest. The darkness has always comforted me—all my life it has been my hiding place. No one could find me in the dark so no one could expect anything from me.

The darkness of night and that of my own humanity were often the only places that I felt safe. It did not matter that for years I believed I did not have a soul, that there was no light within me. I would simply calculate how far I could go into the darkness without getting totally lost, and then wallow at that level for as long as needed before turning around and moving back towards the light of day. In this way, I could manage and control my fear and keep myself safe at the same time. It was not a particularly pleasant way to live, but it worked for me.

However, this trip into darkness was different because Michael was beside me every step of the way. Each time I wanted to pull out of my grief and pain, Michael assured me I was safe. As the darkness became too much for me to bear, his light shone on my next step, never intruding into the pain of the moment nor illuminating anything I was not yet ready to see. Step by step, I descended further into my grief until I reached its final depth and allowed my love for Buddy to flow into the physical world once more. As the light of my love filled the canyon of my grief, I experienced my connection to eternity and realized that while Buddy now resided in the Fairy Realm, we were still connected.

My relationship with Michael also continued to deepen and take on new meaning. While I had recently surrendered my finances to Michael, I had never really allowed him to physically care for me in my day-to-day life on Earth. However, during the most intense periods of my grief, when my mind could not think and my body had no energy to act, Michael had taken care of everything, gently guiding me through each hour of the day. I cherished how clearly I could hear Michael in the silence of my grief, and how safe I felt with his energy wrapped around me twenty-four hours a day.

When I could not care for myself, Michael was there watching over me. My heart was finally filled with the knowledge that I will never have to experience the yearning I sensed within my mother as she searched for her Angel. My Angel and I will continue to share this Earthly life, and when it is time for me to return home, we will be joined there as well.

As I began to pay my monthly bills, I was shocked at how much money I had made without having given my finances a single thought. I realized that my new sense of financial security was not dependent on the amount of my income, but on the knowledge and awareness that I would always be taken care of and have everything I needed in each moment. When I allowed my relationship with Michael and God to completely fulfill me, I discovered that all my fears about money melted away, and I actually wanted less from the outside world.

As my human wants came into alignment with the needs and desires of my Spirit, all forms of abundance—including money, friendships, love, gifts, and opportunities to travel and play—magically flowed into my life.

During the first two months after Buddy died, I repeatedly told Michael how grateful I was for all he was giving me, even though I couldn't feel anything but grief and sadness. Then one day in late October, I thanked Michael for the readings we had done that day and felt the warmth of gratitude flood my entire body. The next day, I felt a moment of happiness and soon after joy.

I was beginning to open my heart again, and the realization that Michael and I were truly partners on the Earth plane made my life much sweeter. By Thanksgiving, I felt a new sense of exhilaration growing within our relationship, and sensed a deep awareness of something new being created within me. It was time to enter Sacred Space and explore the underlying cause of these sensations.

As I entered my valley, I automatically looked for Big Bud, but then remembered he was no longer there. Pink Lady, White, and Yellow greeted me with warm hugs and then guided me across the valley to the base of a small hill where Orange was teaching Purple to shoot flaming arrows into the sky. My first thought was that shooting flaming arrows was not the most appropriate thing to teach a child and we might want Green Guy standing by in case of a mishap! My female essences laughed at my concern and then disappeared as I started up the hill.

I paused at the top of the hill to watch the shooting lesson and immediately noticed that Orange's arrows streamed across the sky with the most beautiful flaming orange color I had ever seen, but when he handed one of his arrows to Purple the flame suddenly turned a deep violet color. I was amazed and asked Purple how she did that. *"It's who I am. I'm not who you think I am."* Purple had said this to me years ago, but I had never understood what she meant. Suddenly, I was very curious and asked, "Who are you?"

"I am Purple of the Violet Flame of Forgiveness. I am your first soul essence and the energy of this lifetime's original Divine Purpose on Earth: FORGIVENESS. For thirteen years, we endured physical pain in order to forgive the Earth's harshness, emotional pain in order to forgive Earth's isolation and separation, and mental pain in order to forgive Earth's creation of fear. When I slipped into the Earth, you lost your ability to forgive yourself, and within a few short years, you forgot how to forgive the world as well.

"Without forgiveness, you were incomplete and fear was able to trap you in your own anger, but it is fear that now trembles at the fire within you. You have taken me back into your heart and released me to the world through the Franz Josef Glacier, and within me lives the full power of the Violet Flame of Forgiveness. The Violet Flame does not destroy anger; it transforms anger into an expression of Divine Love. And without anger, fear will soon become powerless on Earth!

"Forgiveness always precedes peace, so we must complete our original Divine Purpose before you can express the full power of your new energy on Earth. It will be fun. Are you ready?" I was ready, awed, and amazed at what I had just heard. Regardless of her manner and appearance, Purple was not a child!

"I'm ready, what do we do?" Orange handed Purple a pouch filled with flaming arrows, then turned and disappeared into the valley as Purple handed me her bow.

"We forgive."

I felt an anger begin to rise from deep within me as my fingers clenched the shaft of my first arrow. Then I reached out and gently touched Purple's cheek and said, "I forgive you for leaving me."

"I forgive you for letting me go." As I shot the arrow into the sky, I knew that I had just forgiven Purple, Buddy, Mom, and every other

life consciousness that had ever abandoned me on the Earth plane. I continued to shoot an arrow into the sky with each of my intentions to forgive the physical world for taking me away from Michael, creating fear, being so hard, and betraying my innocence. I forgave humanity for pulling me into the belief systems of fear, abusing the natural world, terrifying me, cutting into my body, and exploiting my vulnerabilities.

Then I began to forgive myself for assisting in the deaths of those I loved, for going on without them, for forgetting my Angels and who I really am, for withholding my love from myself and others, for expressing fear, for hurting others, for forgetting my truth, and on and on all afternoon. As dusk began to give way to night, only one flaming arrow remained. I could feel a deep knot in my stomach, but could not grasp its meaning until Purple said, *"You must forgive yourself for falling totally and completely in love with fear."*

I stated my final intent, fired my arrow into the sky, and allowed the Violet Flame of Forgiveness to fully engulf me. A few minutes later, I admitted to Purple that she had been right—that had been fun! We lay on the hilltop and gazed up at the heavens as one by one, our flaming arrows turn into twinkling stars. I knew we had finally healed our past, and in the silence of the night, I embraced a life well lived and accepted my place in the mystery of what was yet to come.

* * *

"It's time to end the book, Little One. The story of your past has reached this moment."

"The book is a memoir; if I end the book, will I die?"

"No."

"If I write a chapter that says I won the lottery, will I win the lottery?"

"No."

"Then how do I end the book?"

"We need to go to Agnes Vaille Falls."

Michael had never taken me to the falls in December, but as I grabbed my snow gear, he assured me we would have no problems getting there. He was right of course; it was one of those warm Colorado days that make you think spring has sprung, but lets you know a big storm is coming tomorrow. When we reached the trailhead, I bundled up and began to climb towards the falls.

The trip took twice as long as usual and I was breathless when I reached the top and heard Michael say, *"You made it!"* I intuitively knew he wasn't talking just about the trek up the mountain. I paused to feel the warmth of the sun on my face and delight in the patterns of color created by the tiny ice crystals that danced all around me. The snow was pure white and its softness muffled the sound of the falling water. I said a prayer of gratitude to Mother Earth before asking, "Why did you bring me here today, Michael?"

"Little One, it is time for you to transcend into Grace and live each moment of your life as it presents itself. You have released the past and are finally ready to give up the future." I felt his words in my heart. One of the things that I was most grateful for in my life was that I did not know about Buddy's cancer sooner. We shared a wonderful spring and summer, but had I known how and when Buddy was leaving, I know my fear would have changed that. I would have cancelled several of our mountain adventures and approached our daily lives with trepidation. I might have even attempted to hold him on Earth longer with uncomfortable medical treatments.

The experiences of the last few months had taught me how impossible it is to plan for the future and how easy it is to live in the moment. Buddy and Michael had reminded me of how little I know and how great are the mysteries I have yet to discover. As I stood on this hallowed ground, I felt my energy begin to rise in anticipation of what was about to be received. My world had waited so long for the manifestation of the Angelic Movement, and until that moment, I had not allowed myself to truly believe it would happen to me in this lifetime.

"The energy that will propel eighty percent of all life consciousness of Earth into the Angelic Movement has already begun to flow into your planet. While the majority of this consciousness currently lies in the natural world, all of humanity will soon begin its journey into the exploration of love on the Earth plane.

"Little One, you made it through the fear. You no longer have to walk through pain to accept, express, and experience love. Your world is finally ready to embrace you, and it is time for you to expand across your planet and allow the colors of your soul to melt into rainbow skies."

As tears of joy began to flow silently from my being, I opened my heart and watched as a rainbow of energy arced out of my chest and melted into the doorway atop the falls. Amidst the ice and snow, I felt the familiar warmth of total peace and fulfillment as the Angelic energy flowed back into my heart. Then suddenly, my existence shifted and I found myself standing not only before Agnes Vaille Falls, but at the base of Melincourt Falls, waist deep in the pool of Cataratas Falls, floating just above the sea floor of Molasses Reef, balancing on the cliffs of Carrington Falls, and perched atop the ice of Franz Josef Glacier. Mother Earth was reaching out from across the entire planet to join me in grace!

I felt the energy of my Spirit as it flowed through DNA handed down to me by countless generations, and embraced life not only as a human, but also as the water, earth, air, fire, and all consciousness of this world. Then from deep within the molten core of this wondrous planet, Purple brought forth the promise of my new journey, *"To forever utilize the colors of my soul to create the doorways, languages, and bridges that will one day allow all humans to walk the Earth with Angels at their side."*

As I began to transcend into a new way of Being, I received an invitation from Mother Earth's most pristine waterfalls, deepest oceans, widest plains, and highest mountains to continue my expansion into the natural world. Instantly, I felt a gentle warmth begin to surge out of every atom of my being. My body, mind, and emotions immediately responded to the tenderness of this energy with a desperate plea to answer Earth's call.

I was plunged back into the fear that my physical limitations would once again deny me a piece of my Divine Path. Overcome by emotions, my mind struggled to prevent my heart from once again shattering into a thousand pieces.

In that moment, I knew that before I could enter into grace and willingly surrender all knowledge of my future, I had to know the answer to one final question, "Michael, will I **EVER** be able to create another matrix with this body?"

"You already have, Little One."

Acknowledgments

My life and this book have grown out of the simple acknowledgment that God's love exists in infinite forms. Without a doubt, Archangel Michael is one of those forms. The pure love and attention of this Angel has allowed me to overcome my fears and doubts, and finally embrace that I too have God's love within me.

I now acknowledge that no matter how farfetched it may seem, everyone and everything on this planet shares this gift with me. I urge everyone who is touched by this book to believe that all those strange coincidences, the blissful dreams, the beautiful colors seen out of the corner of your eyes, those whispers in your heart, that smell that comes from nowhere and that breeze that touches your cheek and hair in the stillness of a room are all Angel connections. It makes no difference whether you are aware or unconscious, a believer or a skeptic—each one of you walks the Earth with Angels.

Michael and I would like to acknowledge your story through mine. We want you to know that every moment of your life is important and the story of your life is more loving and expansive than you will ever know during your stay on Earth. The Angels see you and hear you!

I would also like to acknowledge a few human Angels that helped me with this book. I should not be surprised that those that walk through life with me also walked through the creation of the book with me. Nancy Hart has been there every step of the way, reading each chapter, asking questions, and challenging my thoughts. She helped me write a little book to give to my family and then, along with a friend and client, Megan Bucy, convinced me it was good enough to share with the world.

Courtney Starwolf Barry took my simple idea for the cover and reflected the beauty of the Angelic Realm back to me. Chrys Buckley honored my story and polished it up with a brilliant edit that emphasized the importance of Michael's every word. Chrys actually made me feel like a writer. Terry and Patricia Moore at The Family Studio added to the fun of putting this book together with an amazing photo session and author's photo.

I would also like to thank Joan Schaulbin, Lacy Chupp, and the Balboa staff members for walking me through the publishing process and encouraging me to follow my instincts.

This book is my expression of love to all the ancestors of the new world. Thank you for having the courage to take this journey with me.

About The Author

Viki Hart lives in Colorado Springs, Colorado where in 2006, she discovered that Archangel Michael had moved in with her. She has been channeling for over twenty-four years, and currently provides individual and group Angelic Readings, teaches classes, and travels across the planet opening Angelic Doorways.